Service-Learning

IN HIGHER EDUCATION
AROUND THE WORLD

AN INITIAL LOOK

A report by Howard A. Berry and Linda A. Chisholm
The International Partnership for Service-Learning

with the support of
the Ford Foundation

Schoenbaum Library
University of Charleston
2300 MacCorkle Ave. SE
Charleston, WV 25304

361.37
B459s
1999

Dedicated to the memory of
two pioneers in
international education and service-learning

Luis Garibay Gutiérrez
(1916-1999)

and

Sven Groennings
(1934-1998)

TABLE OF CONTENTS

	Page
Introduction Purpose and extent of the study; sources of information	1
Chapter I - Educators' Reasons Reasons for the initiation and development of service-learning programs	9
Chapter II - Varieties of Service Community needs that students are addressing through service-learning	25
Chapter III - Primary Models Models for linking academic studies to community volunteer service	41
Chapter IV - Related Issues Other issues related to the arranging and organizing of service-learning	53
Chapter V - Institutional Commitment Six outstanding examples from around the world	63
Chapter VI - Present and Future States The state of service-learning at the present, its future, and steps for getting there	81
Appendices	
I Acknowledgments	97
II About the International Partnership	107
III The Wingspread Resolutions, list of signatories	109
IV The Distinguished Partner Program	117
V The National Service Scheme of India	121

INTRODUCTION

In 1998, with the support of the Ford Foundation, The International Partnership for Service-Learning began to survey formally institutions of higher education around the world to determine their interest and involvement in programs that combine academic study and volunteer service.

But in a real sense the investigation began many, many years ago, even before the founding of the Partnership in 1982. Partnership founders had directed two service-learning programs for U.S. students in Africa in the late 1970s. With the birth of the Partnership and the one-by-one creation of its international programs in twelve nations over subsequent years, information was being gathered about student volunteer service, the union of service and formal learning (service-learning), and the attitudes and commitments of institutions of higher education in Africa, the Americas, Asia, Europe, the Middle East, and the then-Soviet Union.

Africa

Africa
Americas
Asia
Europe
Middle East
Soviet Union

As information was gathered directly by the authors of this report, so others involved in the Partnership supplied news of service-learning from the world's nations. Members of the board of trustees, with their extensive international connections, would return from conferences and travels to report on whether service-learning was unknown or commonly practiced in the places they visited. Heads of our affiliated universities similarly reported from their various travels. Partnership program directors in the locations of our programs are knowledgeable about higher education in their region. Reporting on change or lack thereof in the practice of service-learning has been part of the annual meeting of the directors for fifteen years.

From these sources of information, we concluded that in the early 1980s and throughout the decade, volunteer community service was not seen as an important source for learning by institutions of higher education around the world. There were notable exceptions, such as the Universidad Autónoma de Guadalajara in Mexico and Trinity College of Quezon City in the Philippines, whose experience with academic programs of service in the community was decades old.

Mexico
Philippines

Then in the early 1990s it seemed to the Partnership staff at the headquarters in New York and to our partners in affiliated colleges, universities, and service agencies abroad that service-learning was springing up spontaneously and independently in many regions of the world. Although called by a variety of names, including "extension education" (India), "study service" (United Kingdom), "practical education" (Uganda), "social service course" (Korea), "work-study" (Jamaica), and "programs of education in the community" (Mexico), the practice of joining formal education with volunteer community service was gaining a foothold in higher education in many parts of the world. And the very phrase "service-learning," which a decade earlier had been mistaken as a description of learning for the *armed* services or as referring somehow to the idea of the service *economy*, began to bring glimmers of recognition. The pedagogy of joining the experience of volunteer service to formal learning was undergoing a noticeable change.

India
United Kingdom
Uganda
Korea
Jamaica
Mexico

Institutions of higher education in widely divergent cultures and systems were finding in service-learning a means of addressing the ills of both communities and education. As we talked with educators, we discovered a commonality of concern. In one month's time we visited a teachers' college in the mountains of Jamaica and an institute of technology in Taiwan. The facilities, student profiles, and resources of these two institutions could not have been more different. But the similarity of language used by the respective heads to describe the ways in which education is failing was notable. Even more striking, they were agreed on what was needed and how volunteer service brought into the very heart of the educational mission of the institution could reinvigorate and redirect learning.

Jamaica
Taiwan

Conversations with service agency personnel revealed similarities as well. Communities in nations rich and poor are facing the same issues—failing educational systems, joblessness, reduction of available health care, drug use and trafficking, dysfunctional families, neglected children and elderly, inadequate services for the handicapped, teenage delinquency, and destruction of the environment. Most of these agencies were actively seeking volunteers to assist in their mission, recognizing that college and university students are an important potential source of help for their work.

Throughout these conversations with educators and service providers ran the theme of misunderstanding and conflict among people of different ethnic origins, religious beliefs, races, classes, economic circumstances, nationalities and cultures.

Wanting to know more about what was happening with regard to service-learning around the world and how the International Partnership might assist the growing service-learning movement, in May of 1998 we convened an international meeting at the Wingspread Conference Center in Wisconsin, United States. With the support of the Ford Foundation and the Johnson Foundation, forty-two high-level educators and service providers met to report on the state of service–learning in their nations and regions and to consider what might be done to bolster the efforts that were, for the most part, as yet but fledgling. They came from sixteen nations—the Czech Republic, Denmark, Ecuador, England, France, Hong Kong (soon to be the People's Republic of China), India, Indonesia, Jamaica, Jordan, the Lakota Nation (of the U.S.), Liberia, Mexico, the Philippines, Scotland, South Africa and the United States.

Furthermore, many of the delegates represented international organizations such as the Association of African Universities (100 members); the International Association of University Presidents (600); the United Board for Christian Higher Education in Asia (74 colleges and universities in twelve Asian nations); Colleges

Czech Republic
Denmark
Ecuador
England
France
Hong Kong
India
Indonesia
Jamaica
Jordan
Lakota Nation (U.S.)
Liberia
Mexico
Philippines
Scotland
South Africa
United States

and Universities of the Anglican Communion (120 colleges and universities in twenty nations), and Peer Tutoring International. The United States was represented by the executive director of Campus Compact, an organization promoting volunteer service and service-learning in over 500 U.S. colleges and universities. From their extensive and collective experience, the Wingspread Conference participants (listed in Appendix 3) added greatly to our understanding of what was and was not happening in various areas of the world, and which forces were promoting or preventing the development of service-learning.

Soon after the conference we sent a formal questionnaire to institutions around the world with which we had had contact in one way or another, either directly or through related umbrella organizations. Sixty-four institutions of higher education in twenty-three nations responded. From our contacts we obtained detailed descriptions of service-learning in another thirty-three institutions, bringing the total number of colleges and universities to ninety-seven and the number of countries to thirty-two. Experts in higher education in other parts of the world supplied general information about their areas and regions. (See Appendix 1 for a listing of those persons, institutions, and organizations supplying information.)

The institutions from which we have gathered information for this report represent an array of public and private, large and small, old and prestigious and young and struggling institutions of higher education. Their student bodies are made up of every major religious affiliation (Muslim, Christian, Hindu, Buddhist, and Jewish) or no such affiliation; their curricula range from those exclusively focused on career preparation to those teaching only the liberal arts.

East and Southeast Asia
North and South America
Caribbean
Europe
Eastern Europe
Africa
Middle East

In all, the state of service-learning in higher education has been described in institutions of higher education in East and Southeast Asia, including India; in North and South America and the Caribbean; in Europe, including Eastern Europe; and in Africa and the Middle East, including both Israel and predominantly Muslim nations.

There are of course vast differences in educational systems, missions, curricula, student bodies, faculty expertise, histories, resources and the cultural patterns of the societies supporting these institutions of higher education. And service agencies can be found which advocate the widest range of philosophies, missions, and methods, and which, like colleges and universities, have vastly different resources with which to address problems. Students express a range of motivations and goals and demonstrate an infinite variety of talents, limitations and interests. Still, despite these differences, there is a common concern for the world and its people as we approach the new millennium, one that the union of higher learning with community service seems to be addressing.

We have put together the information thus gathered into this report. It is of course only an initial look. We know—and indeed rejoice—that the document is out of date the moment it is sent to the printer. New information arrives daily about institutions and agencies that are joining forces to revitalize learning in its many dimensions and to address problems of communities, nations, and the world.

The information contained in the report makes no claim to be complete, nor representative, nor quantitative. A statistical study of service-learning worldwide would be encyclopedic, for there are thousands upon thousands of institutions of higher education and many times that number of service agencies.

However, we have been able to sort out the primary motivations and models in use in the institutions with which we are familiar, citing examples of service-learning programs and the interest in service-learning around the world. We hope and expect that other models and examples will be uncovered in the months and years ahead. (If you have knowledge of service-learning, we would be most grateful to you for information that might one day be included in *A Second Look!*)

We add here a note on language usage in this report. From nation to nation, and indeed between different regions and subcultures within each nation, language usage varies greatly. In an effort to preserve authenticity, we have reproduced the words, phrases, and spellings as they appear in the returned surveys and other communications.

We were given energy to conduct the study and issue this report by the thousands of young people from twenty-two nations who have been participants in the service-learning programs of The International Partnership for Service-Learning and by the many more whom we have met in our visits to colleges and universities around the world. They have in common hope and idealism which have always been the special property of the young. We admire—and sometimes envy—their eagerness to be tested; their passion for justice; their willingness to make personal sacrifices for the good of others; their intelligence in analyzing problems and imagining solutions; their joy; their confidence in themselves and the future; and their humility as they work for and with others, usually their own countrymen, who are facing monumental problems. As they learn and serve, we watch them develop into strong, knowledgeable, caring and wise leaders.

Scotland

Liberia

We have been renewed by the stories we have found from various institutions. There are those, such as the University of Glasgow, whose history and prestige would have allowed them to rest on their laurels but who are forging new ground through service-learning. And there are those—like Cuttington University in Liberia, struggling to serve its nation as it rebuilds after a decade of devastating civil war—that have meager resources and yet are extending what they have for the good of the wider community.

This small volume, then, is meant to help you realize, wherever you are, that across cultures there is a commonality among seekers who are troubled by the social and educational problems before them. We hope you will find encouragement from these seekers who are finding that joining service and learning is a powerful combination for reforming education and addressing needs that would otherwise remain unmet.

It is our hope that, in seeing this report and knowing that there are individuals and institutions around the world creating this especially rich and socially useful form of education, teachers in many nations will be encouraged to explore service-learning and to look beyond their own borders for examples to replicate; service agencies will welcome students to aid their work and will share with them their rich body of knowledge; students will know and have contact with their counterparts around the world as they learn about and tackle needs; and philanthropists and funding agencies in many nations will open their purses to provide scholarship money and institutional support for this emerging form of education.

It took over one hundred years for the laboratory method to be accepted as the standard way for the natural sciences to be taught. We hope the acceptance of service-learning will not take so long. Our study, modest though it is, describes a worldwide movement in higher education that is gathering momentum and numbers, a movement that with encouragement and support can make real, lasting differences in education and society, and in the lives of those serving as well as those being served.

Howard A. Berry   Linda A. Chisholm
President   Vice President

New York City, July, 1999

CHAPTER I

EDUCATORS' REASONS

Educators around the world cite various reasons or a combination of reasons for developing and supporting programs of service-learning. Overarching is their realization that colleges and universities must find means of reconnecting or connecting more fully with their communities, nations, and the world. They are aware that the problems societies face are not one-dimensional. The inextricable links between problems such as jobs, housing, and education demand that the resources of varying organizations and social institutions be brought to bear in a coordinated way for problems to be successfully addressed, suffering alleviated, development undertaken, conflicts peaceably resolved, and justice brought closer to realization. Kevin Bales,[1] a principal lecturer at the Roehampton Institute London of the University of Surrey, in England, put it this way: *England*

> My career has been spent oscillating between the academic world and the voluntary sector. From that perspective it is clear how much they have to offer each other. The intellectual power of universities is often squandered on the unintelligible and the irrelevant. The energies of communities can be dissipated in earnest but unreflective enthusiasm. Strategic thought and analysis joined to community vision and power can change lives for the better.

Local, national and international problems have an impact on colleges and universities, and educators are acknowledging and accepting the responsibilities they have for leadership in the society. Colin Bundy, vice-chancellor of the University of

---

1. Except where noted, all of those quoted in Chapter I were invited participants in the Wingspread Conference and all quotations are taken from statements made during the conference or in biographical information submitted prior to the conference.

South Africa Witwatersrand in Johannesburg, South Africa, described the changing role of universities:

> No university is an ivory tower—even if it wishes to be. Universities are deeply implicated in the modern state and are key agents of modern society. This means that they should be conscious of, and make choices about, the *terms* of that involvement. Universities can be the brains and the skilled hands of their immediate community; but they can also be the conscience, the source of reflection, and a shaping imagination for change. Higher education *must* be critically engaged in the needs of communities, nations, and the world: not least because it may just be the last, best hope that communities, nations and the world have for considering what, why and how they do things.

Among the specific issues for which college and university leaders are assuming their share of responsibility and that they declare are reasons for engaging their students and faculty in programs linking service and learning are:

EDUCATION REFORM

Encompassing all of the specific reasons for instituting service-learning is that of the reform of higher education in mission, structures, pedagogy and outcomes. Thoughtful educators are recalling that the great and historic purpose of higher learning in many different cultures and traditions was to provide skilled leaders for the society. They declare that there is a need for an educated citizenry with a broad appreciation of the world and its issues; who recognize that their own understanding, experience, mindset and beliefs are not universal; and who possess the skills to negotiate differences and work out equitable arrangements for the social order. They cite their college mottoes, emblazoned above doorways and upon the college seal; Payap University in Chiang Mai, Thailand, is but one of the hundreds of colleges with the motto of "truth and service."

Thailand

Educators criticize the specialization, fragmentation and isolation of knowledge through division into disciplines and departments. They worry that compartmentalization allows too little dialogue between faculty members and between the university and the community that surrounds it. They see students who mistake the theoretical constructs of a discipline or field with reality itself, students who fail to see that theories and methodologies are merely a way to order complex and often contradictory information. And they lament that students, taught to believe that schooling is the only source of learning, are unable to learn from the first and primary teacher—experience.

In the face of the new technologies, educators are asking how colleges and universities should be reshaped. The factory model of higher education fashioned in the nineteenth century seems sadly out of sync with the modern world. The process that puts students on a kind of conveyor belt to be worked on by successive specialists until at the end of the line they are duly stamped with the proper credentials does not prepare them for the new, active and interactive world outside the academy. But adequate pedagogies for teaching the sophisticated skills for analyzing, evaluating and using the information that comes pell-mell over the World Wide Web have yet to be developed.

Even more alarming to some educators is the question of the socialization of students. Colleges and universities have always provided an interim stage between childhood and adulthood. How are institutions of higher education to provide the environment and direction that will help students to become mature and responsible adults? Prezell Robinson, president emeritus of St. Augustine's College, in North Carolina, United States, and a former public delegate from the United States to the United Nations, summarized the issue this way: "The world we knew twenty-five years ago has figuratively shrunk about twenty-five percent or more. The international information highway and distance learning all have brought us closer to each other. Now, we must learn to live with each other."

United States

Finally, when educators talk of the need for education reform, they inevitably refer to the global connections that, whether through technology, travel, commerce or other institutions of society, characterize the world at the close of the twentieth century. They acknowledge that the essential isolation of colleges and universities from one another as separate fiefdoms is anachronistic in today's world, rendering higher education all but powerless to act as a force for good in the modern world.

THE DEVELOPMENT OF HUMANE VALUES

Educators recognize that higher education has had, over centuries of history and tradition, a number of purposes including the transmission of cultural heritage, the training of professionals, and the generation of new knowledge through research. But many educators are stating unequivocally that foremost among the purposes is that of giving young adults the skills and breadth of knowledge to think deeply about the structures of their society and to appropriate values which must govern their personal and professional lives. Higher learning is equated with ethical and honorable behavior and acceptance of the notion that the privilege of education also carries with it responsibility for the welfare for those not so privileged. One of India's most renowned educators, Mithra Augustine, expressed eloquently the thoughts of all at Wingspread:

India

> The role and function of universities and colleges were earlier seen as integral to the processes of social engineering, developing in students critical faculties, creative potential and initiative towards applying these to the tasks of freeing people from material want and intellectual deprivation. Amidst current trends of modernisation and globalisation the culture of self-interest is growing dominant in centres of higher education. The interest is in training for lucrative careers at the expense of all else once supportive of social concerns of justice, peace, and integrity of creation.

One related issue of deep concern has been the role that higher education has played in condoning, and being the means for, the move of many graduates up and out of their home communities and even their nations. This "brain drain" is a reality whether the move is from a rural village to an urban center or from a developing nation to one in the First World. Florence McCarthy, professor of international education development at Teachers College, Columbia University, in the U.S., chastised: *United States*

> To date, higher education has generally not seen its role as being linked to those of everyday people, and the long traditions of privilege and elitism which are embodied in these institutions mean they often are unsympathetic to the fate of the majority of their people. The provision of knowledge to those in need of it, as well as the direction of research and teaching to serve the needs of local people rather than the needs of global corporations or foreign interests, are pressing problems for the next century. There is a great need for new thinking and action in forging new partnerships with communities and civic and social organizations to work for the delivery of justice and respect along with food, clothing, shelter and other basic needs.

Many university heads agree with Professor McCarthy, admitting to the role their institutions have played in making possible this flight to personal advancement at the expense of those left behind. And they are seeking ways to change this damaging   *Philippines*
effect of higher education. In the Philippines, Silliman University's program is designed to encourage education students to remain in rural areas as teachers. The programs of American College in Madurai, India, "enable the town-bred students   *India*
to have experience with the realities of rural life and the rural-bred students to have opportunities to share their knowledge with their kith and kin."[2]

Above all, educators express a deep concern about the materialism that has gripped societies around the world at the expense of the common good. Consumerism, which uses precious resources needed by many merely for survival, and financial success built on disregard for the rights and needs of workers and

---

2. From the returned survey.

the larger community are cited as rampant within rich and poor nations alike. Educators, while certainly not opposed to business and commerce per se, are calling for a countervailing voice to promote values that respect the wider needs and emphasize a common life as people of one world. Nicholas Taylor, the executive director of the Joint Education Trust in South Africa, said succinctly, "We need to develop a service ethic in a society increasingly dominated by material values."

South Africa

LEADERSHIP

Closely related to the issue of developing humane values is that of developing leaders whose primary concern is for the welfare of others and for the common good. Although in virtually all parts of the world opportunity for higher education is expanding with more students from a wider variety of backgrounds having access, it remains true that in almost all nations only a small percentage of young people can aspire to higher education. And it is true that most local, national, and world leaders are those among those so privileged. Education is the key to leadership positions. Colleges and universities know that their graduates will go forth into roles in which they will be models and will determine the policies guiding and governing their societies in the years ahead. Adel Safty of Egypt was formerly the head of the United Nations University International Leadership Academy which has headquarters in Jordan, and he is now director of the larger Centre for Global Leadership. He contrasts the prevailing definition of leadership development as that of training for effective management of corporations with that of leadership education in "the skills and attitudes which will support sustainable development, sustainable democracy, civil society and the peaceful resolution of disputes." Thoughtful educators, knowledgeable about history, speak of the distinctions between the qualities of leaders who have contributed positively to the good of society and those who have used their positions of power for destructive ends. As our century of violence comes to a close, they express the hope that their institutions will fos-

Egypt

Jordan

ter the characteristics of a true statesman and community servant-leader. Rance Lee, the head of Chung Chi College of the Chinese University of Hong Kong, China, wrote:

China

> Most students have become individualist as well as materialistic. From my contacts with major universities in the Chinese mainland, similar changes in student culture have also taken place there. I am disappointed to see such changes among the future leaders...Perhaps this is a worldwide trend. It appears that globalization has made the world become smaller, but it has also made people become less human. I want to find ways to re-shape the student orientations. I hope that all institutions of higher education around the world come to join forces in building up humanitarian values among leaders of future generations.

CITIZENSHIP

For many educators, nurturing citizens who will be full participants in the democratic process is a primary impetus for their commitment to service-learning. In the United States and nations of Europe there is growing concern about the lack of involvement and even interest in the operations of government. The reluctance to vote in elections and the unwillingness to consider ever running for political office leaves educators wondering who will be governing in the future and who will be monitoring the policies of government officials. Louis Albert, who at the time of the Wingspread Conference was the vice president of the American Association for Higher Education, declared, "Preparing the next generation for a lifelong commitment to productive citizenship is the most important challenge facing educators and communities at the local, regional, national, and global levels. How education can do this best is my highest priority."

United States
Europe

In developing countries and emerging democracies, the mood is no less urgent. Carmen Pencle, a senior lecturer at the University of Technology in Jamaica, testified to the importance of service-learning: "Students are being educated for social recon-

Jamaica

struction and community service is one important way of preparing them for this task." P. Pandiyaraja, vice principal of American College in Madurai, India, has written:[3]

India

> Adult illiteracy is a major problem. Since all adults have voting rights, adult illiteracy programmes enhance the quality of the functioning of democracy in our country. Also, this creates awareness of other issues like the environment, health and human rights.

Involving students in service and using their experience as a means of asking questions about the role of government in providing for the common welfare is one important means of raising up a new generation who will understand the functioning of political systems and their relation to the needs of the people they govern.

CROSS-CULTURAL COMMUNICATION

Societies around the world experience divisions by class, ethnicity and religion, economic circumstance, and educational achievement. In some places, these differences have developed into hostilities of discord, civil unrest, sporadic violence, and even full-scale war. In others, there is an underlying fear that the chasms between people are growing and will one day be too large to bridge. Even in nations such as Denmark that have traditionally been homogeneous, new populations of immigrants are exposing the conflicts that arise when diverse cultures are brought together with little understanding of one another. The movement of peoples and the recognition of the formerly unseen and voiceless are making educators aware that they must find ways of teaching students to live together in harmony. Willi Toisuta, an advisor to the president of Pelita Harapan University in Jakarta, Indonesia, stated:

Denmark

Indonesia

---

3. From the returned survey.

The knowledge, expertise and skills in higher learning institutions should be made available at any time to meet community needs through outreach programs. In a wider context, international exchange and cooperation through higher education will narrow the gap between nations and thus improve understanding between peoples so as to promote the culture of peace.

Educators are trying a variety of means for addressing these issues, including opening the doors of educational opportunity to a wider and more diverse population. They are also seeking ways of educating their students to the beliefs, points of view and life circumstances of those different from themselves. While traditional classroom-based study of cultures, languages and social conditions remains a primary means by which universities educate about differences, there are those who believe that it is actual contact which deepens and extends the appreciation, empathy and compassion they seek to engender. Humphrey Tonkin, president emeritus of the University of Hartford in the United States, wrote:

United States

> My interest in service-learning springs from a deep conviction that the future of our increasingly commingled and fluid world society depends on an ability to understand difference, and to manage it. In the process, we must soften the extremes that lead to conflict and develop a willingness on the part of all people to step out of themselves and see things from other people's points of view.

Liberia

Melvin Mason, the president of Cuttington University College in Liberia, agreed:

> Connecting higher education to communities, nations and the world is very important because at this level students realize that problems are global in character, and their solutions require understanding, appreciating and respecting racial, ethnic, cultural and religious differences. Moreover, higher education exposes one to all the theories about a new world order, but it is connecting the various facets of society and providing the environment for positive interaction that makes a positive difference.

Chapter I

THEORY AND PRACTICE

As educators like Humphrey Tonkin and Melvin Mason realize that cross-cultural appreciation and skills are best learned by a combination of classroom study and direct encounter with the people of another culture, so educators around the globe are increasingly finding ways to credit experiential education in general and service-learning in particular for the mastering of a variety of skills. Nirmala Jeyaraj, the principal of Lady Doak College in India, applauded the opportunity "to apply what is learned in the classroom to real life situations, and thereby to be provided the chance for case studies and personal interviews in areas related to gender, environment and health issues." Descriptions of the programs of Central Philippine University in Iloilo, express the values shared by many educators of problem-centered learning and teaching. "[This pedagogy of service-learning] is the most conducive to the building of substantive knowledge for the fostering of an exploratory and inventive disposition in students and teachers, and to the transfer and continuing use of learning."[4]

India

Philippines

Professional education such as nursing, social work, and teaching have long considered experience integral and essential to preparation in their fields. But in recent years the notion of what may be better learned through experience has been extended. Understanding ethics, for example, may best be understood by combining classroom study with experience in a service agency which daily must decide who of the needy will be served and who must be refused. Professors of literature, such as Veta Lewis, who is the head of the technical education department of the University of Technology in Jamaica, have found their subject enlivened for students who are meeting, in the service they perform, people whose lives parallel or contrast with the lives of characters in the novels they are assigned for reading and classroom discussion.

Jamaica

---

4. Material from the department of social work, sent with the returned survey.

Sven Caspersen, the rector of Aalborg University in Denmark, which is famous for its engineering studies, has written: *Denmark*

> As head of a university I have found it important to encourage initiatives which help increase the cooperation between the university and the surrounding society—whether regionally, nationally or globally. At the same time I have found it important that the cooperation between the university and the surrounding society should not only be of an economic, technological and social nature, but should also be based on cultural, humanistic and ethical values which should be an active part of the studies both as regards contents and the interactions between theory and practice.

Fieldwork in disciplines including sociology and anthropology, which once were observational only, has been extended to include active service. Teachers in these fields are recognizing that simply studying a people without interacting with them at the same time is a form of exploitation, and that the active participant has access to information which observation alone cannot provide.

Rex Taylor, of the University of Glasgow, in Scotland, summarized the dissatisfaction that educators are feeling and to which they are reacting by advocating service-learning: *Scotland*

> One of the defects of the modern world is the divorce between knowledge and experience. Those with knowledge and learning often have little experience of the world, and those with worldly experience have but limited knowledge and feeble imaginations. The function of the University should be to marry knowledge with experience so that classroom-based learning is enriched by experiential learning. Service learning is an ideal way of achieving this marriage."

INSTITUTIONAL MISSION

For many colleges and universities around the world, service to the wider community has been part of the institutional mission and heritage since the time of their founding. First among these are institutions with religious foundations. The hundreds of colleges and universities around the world founded by a branch of the Christian church have had at the heart of their mission the extension of educational opportunity to those previously denied access. In the early years of many of these institutions of higher education, admission was given to the poor and disenfranchised. The distinguished St. John's College in Agra, India, among the first in India to admit as students those of the untouchable caste, is such an example. The colleges making up Roehampton Institute London, of the University of Surrey, in England, were founded in the nineteenth century to provide trained teachers for the newly opening schools for poor and working children. Women's colleges throughout the world, like Stella Maris College and Lady Doak College in India, some operated by religious orders, had as their purpose the raising up of women.

India

England

In other locations the founding of the college or university corresponded to the independence of the nation and the need to serve the emerging nation and society. Ben Gurion University in Israel and the University of Technology in Jamaica are but two of the hundreds of examples that might be here cited.

Israel
Jamaica

Some institutions were established in response to political change. The Universidad Autónoma de Guadalajara was the first private university in Mexico. It was founded in the 1930s out of opposition to the communist influence at the public university, and from the beginning integrated community service into the curriculum. These programs of education in the community were a demonstration of the founders' commitment to serve the community but in a way different from the prevailing political party's notion about how services should be provided to the people of the region. Trinity College of Quezon City, in the Philippines, was created to provide education to those fleeing guerrilla action in northern Luzon and, like the Universidad Autónoma de Guadalajara, instituted service as an example of community cooperation.

Mexico

Philippines

Today the historic mission of these institutions is finding expression in outreach programs. St. John's College and Lady Doak College, for example, have made the development of village women a major college commitment. Ben Gurion University works extensively on behalf of new immigrants from North Africa and Russia. Students at Trinity College of Quezon City serve in the squatters' communities in Manila. Students at the Universidad Autónoma de Guadalajara serve the city and surrounding towns through medical and legal clinics for the poor, as teachers in schools of all kinds, and through a wide variety of other social service projects.

India
Israel

Philippines

Mexico

STUDENT INTEREST AND DEMAND

Finally, educators are responding through service-learning programs to their students' interest in human problems and their desire to be of use. Restlessness with "the endless snare of preparation" and the "longing to construct the world anew" are traits belonging especially to the young, and no generation or nation is without its idealists.[5] In seeking programs of service and learning, students around the world share the sentiments of the few here quoted.[6]

> Since I entered school, I have always been busy studying and doing homework....I had no chance to participate in any kind of public service activities and I badly regret it....I want to be of great help to people who need me. Service-learning will lead me to learn and feel what I should do to help others materially and psychologically. This will be my touchstone through my life and lead me to a sound foundation.
> Lee Soo Hyu, Korea

Korea

---

5. The Wingspread Conference was entitled "Constructing the World Anew," a quotation taken from the autobiography of Jane Addams, a prominent American social reformer of the late nineteenth and early twentieth century. For her leadership in the settlement house movement serving new immigrants, Jane Addams was awarded the Nobel Peace Prize in 1935. In *My Twenty Years at Hull House*, she wrote of her young adult life, "I was restless with the endless snare of preparation and I was longing to construct the world anew."

6. Quoted from student applicants and participants in programs of the Partnership.

Nigeria

Service-learning gives me a first-hand experience of team work and brings me in contact with people, especially children. I consider this vital because I want to be a doctor.

Ifeoma Nnaji, Nigeria

Japan

I would like not only to study sitting at my desk but also to go to the place, to touch and feel…and to think about the problems more deeply and practically.

Miyuki Araki, Japan

I have done a lot of thinking in the last few years about what I want to do with my life (what student has not?) and the conclusion that I have come to is that although academic knowledge is important, it means nothing by itself. I feel that however many books I read, however much knowledge I accumulate, it will be meaningless unless I actually *do* something which has significance for someone's life. Action is so much more important than words. To sit in a classroom discussing world problems without ever trying to contribute to their solutions is hypocritical and ineffectual. This is not to say that academic studies are unimportant. On the contrary, they are important because knowledge is a powerful tool for combating problems and injustices. However, theories must be applied to determine their usefulness….Actions give life meaning, and knowing that life is uncertain from one day to the next, I don't want to wait until some vague future date to begin *doing* something.

United States

Tanya Dean, United States

Colombia

Through service-learning, I will gain knowledge while giving everything I have to offer to others.

Rosemary Vargas, Colombia

Hungary

In service-learning, I meet a lot of interesting people and as much as I teach them, they teach me just as much.

Bernadett Palfray, Hungary

In University, I have tried to complement my academic studies with volunteer experiences, to be able to see and actually experience…what I only read about in my textbooks at school, crucial in enhancing my learning.…In doing so, I can build a more solid foundation of knowledge and skills so that ultimately I can be a more effective person.

Canada

Janice Tulling, Canada

IN CONCLUSION

Educators around the world are returning to the age-old questions of higher learning—its purpose, its content, the pedagogy for delivery, and the outcomes. What defines the educated person? What ought he or she to know, to understand, to be able to do, to believe? Will we know the educated person by his or her attitudes, approaches, and actions? How will we teach so that our graduates acquire these characteristics?

The joining of formal learning and volunteer community service interests educators because it seems to them a means of addressing these central issues of education simultaneously. Most reforms proposed for education identify a single weakness and seek to correct it through a single method. Service-learning has captured the imagination of educators precisely because it is a way of focusing attention on the several issues outlined above. While not providing the answer to all of the world's or education's ills, service-learning is proving to these educators and to hundreds of others around the world the power to bring social and intellectual problems into the light of day. There they are subject to scrutiny by students, by faculty, and by the community, each of whom may see the issues differently. Service-learning demands the examination of values, fosters leadership, stimulates community involvement, requires cross-cultural interaction, gives programmatic expression to the rhetoric of institutional mission statements, and enlivens learning.

Answering so very many criticisms of higher education and offering such promise as the means for re-forming education, it is no wonder that service-learning is capturing respect and commitment around the world. Having gathered such momentum, service-learning now deserves recognition as a worldwide movement.

CHAPTER II

VARIETIES OF SERVICE

Students around the world engaged in service-learning programs are addressing a wide variety of human and community needs. Of the myriad social problems facing communities, some lend themselves naturally to the interests and skills of college and university students, fitting well with the curricula, schedule, and mission of the educating institution.

TEACHING

Teaching is foremost among the ways students can and do contribute to communities. Literacy and numeracy are skills that every student in higher education possesses and help in teaching these skills is needed by communities in affluent areas as well as developing ones. In South Africa, students at the University of Witwatersrand, in Johannesburg, are putting to use their own recently-honed skills by tutoring under-prepared black high school students for their university entrance examinations. In the United States, college and university students routinely tutor their fellow students who, admitted provisionally to the institution, are in need of remedial help. *South Africa*

United States

In school settings, service-learning students in almost every country surveyed are teaching or working as teachers' assistants in preschools, elementary and secondary schools. Where class sizes are large, students go from child to child, tutoring, checking lessons and giving encouragement. As they serve the children, so they serve the teachers by relieving them of routine tasks, monitoring the playground and lunchroom and being there for the teacher who otherwise would have to choose between attending to the needs of the class or those of an individual child.

In some cases, students bring skills in art, music, drama or sports, instructing in those subjects that because of budget limitations cannot be taught by professional teachers. Mexico and Jamaica are but two of the nations in which agencies are using university students in this way. Of special note is the skill of today's university students in the use of computers. Schools around the world are acquiring hardware and software that current teachers may not themselves know how to operate. College students in these cases become tutors to both children and teachers. St. John's and St. Mary's Institute of Technology in Taiwan is initiating a service-learning program in which students will teach computer use and maintenance.

Mexico
Jamaica

Taiwan

One of the most extensive school tutoring programs is in Great Britain, where the Peer Tutoring Scheme places thousands of students from over fifty universities as tutors in the local schools. It was begun in 1975 at Imperial College, an independent constituent of University of London. Named "The Pimlico Connection," the program sent students into local schools to work in the classroom under the direction of the professional teachers. Students helped with group work, sometimes giving demonstrations, and assisted in classes with children of mixed abilities. The Imperial College program gained the attention and support of British Petroleum, which later expanded support to other universities wanting to establish similar programs. Now British Petroleum has established the BP International Tutoring and Mentoring Project sponsoring regional and international conferences and supporting schemes in Europe, Africa, Australia, Malaysia and Singapore.

Great Britain

Europe
Africa
Australia
Malaysia
Singapore

The Peer Tutoring Scheme is noteworthy not only for its extent but also for two other aspects. It is not a teacher training program but rather it engages as tutors and mentors students planning other careers, and it encourages the participation of the many foreign students who have come to Britain to study in the university.

In addition to primary- and secondary-school programs, students are serving in other academic settings. They are teaching literacy, numeracy and second languages to adults in evening programs, and job skills to the able-bodied as well as the disabled.

Hospitals and residential homes for children and adults with handicapping conditions are using students to complement their often meager professional staffs. Linden House for the Blind in London is but one of thousands of such homes finding that the encouragement and attention which service-learning students are able to give is a valuable ingredient in a child's adjustment and progress. In Guayaquil, Ecuador, students from the Universidad Espíritu Santo have provided dance classes at the hospital for children with mental problems. Students at Charles University in Prague, Czech Republic, offer music and other enrichment programs for children with mental disabilities.

England

Ecuador

Czech Republic

Students at St. John's College in Palayamkottai, India, go regularly to work with children at the nearby residential home for the Deaf and Dumb School. College Principal J. Balasingh reported in his survey that the children are well cared for at the home by a benevolent staff and efficient management.

India

> Yet this large section of boys and girls do have—it is quite natural—a feeling of insecurity and dissatisfaction in social life. Our student volunteers had devoted their time and energy to drive away from [the children's] minds these feelings of insecurity and dissatisfaction. They had striven hard to inculcate and foster a sense of equality, security and satisfaction in their minds by understanding certain activities. They rendered their services around the clock. Fifty boys and twenty girls have already devoted their heart and soul to this field of social service. They have visited the school almost all days. Some of them taught the boys needing extra help in subjects in the evenings; some helped them in dining halls; some made them participate in social gatherings outside the school; still others gave the children training in games and sports. These and other activities have gone a long way [in boosting their self esteem] in social life and in making their lives happy and content.

Important though they are, schools are but one of the educating institutions in society. Countless programs exist that seek to enrich and deepen the learning that takes place in school settings or to give new or different knowledge, skills, or values. Organizations such as Boy Scouts, Girl Guides, the YMCA, service organizations, sports clubs, churches and synagogues are only a few of the hundreds of organizations which depend on university students such as those at King Alfred's College in Winchester, England, to staff their programs. Students of Sarah Tucker College in Tamil Nadu, India, go regularly to the Videvelli Ashram to teach Sunday classes to children and the weekly lesson to the students of the ashram. At Lady Doak in India, students tutor the children of support staff of the college.

England
India

Some of these programs seek to fill the needs of the poorest and most disadvantaged of a society. Often combining teaching with feeding and health care, these programs serve children who live in the streets, who work, whose parents are in prison or who must work long hours away from home (thereby leaving them alone). When middle- or upper-class university students such as those at Universidad San Francisco de Quito (USFQ), Ecuador, work in such programs, they find them demanding, challenging, eye-opening, and ultimately deeply rewarding. One USFQ student wrote:

Ecuador

> Perhaps I couldn't change the lives of these people who spend their lives just surviving, in a constant battle against loneliness and poverty, but I can say that they changed my life....One part of me awoke, a part that was disconnected from the real world and that lived in a kind of bubble listening to and seeing the problems of others as if they had nothing to do with me. I realized that the pain of others is also mine and that I cannot be completely happy if there is someone who asks for my hand and I do not do anything about it.

In addition to the specific knowledge and skills university students bring to their formal and informal teaching, they also bring the example of their own lives. Most university students have learned the self-discipline required for educational achievement and are able to get along positively and productively with others. Children and adolescents look up to these young adults, who are usually closer to them in age than their professional teachers or agency supervisors. As university students serve in educational programs they are admired and imitated, often without their being aware of this important way of serving. School heads, teachers, and agency personnel express their delight and gratitude when they see their charges patterning themselves after these heroes in their lives. Educators and social-service providers find their work strengthened when university students are present to serve as desirable role models.

One of the most interesting observations of school and agency supervisors is that students play a valuable role by being recognized as outside the usual lines of authority. In Scotland, for example, students at the University of Glasgow encourage parents who did not finish school themselves to participate in the school activities of their children. Suspicious of teachers and social workers, these parents will agree to go with the university student who invites and accompanies them to school functions and for meetings with their children's teachers. Similar results are reported from programs with juvenile offenders and others who need a friend and advocate who is not in a position to decide their fate. *Scotland*

Many universities and organizations around the world make service and learning in another country possible, and when they do their students find themselves teaching about their own culture. A decade ago, students from the United States, serving and learning in Mexico, became the first teachers at an elementary school in an underserved community. The first of these students made a large map of the Americas. Each successive volunteer and any visitors pinpoint their home community and describe it to the children. Students from Ewha University who go on school-sponsored service programs to Bangladesh, China, Nepal, or Russia, teach about their native Korea. *United States*

Korea

While much cross-cultural teaching is cross-national, there are opportunities within students' own countries. Ben Gurion University students are teaching about the government and culture of Israel to those newly arrived from former Soviet countries and from North Africa. Students at Macalester College in St. Paul, Minnesota, in the U.S., help to prepare immigrants for citizenship examinations. At Petra University in Indonesia, students from urban centers serve in the villages learning about rural culture and teaching about city and suburban life. Whether the teaching is formal or informal these students of higher education around the world are preparing others as they themselves are being prepared to live and work in a cross-cultural world that is now part of the lives of people everywhere and in all circumstances.

Israel

United States
Indonesia

HEALTH CARE

A second area in which thousands of college and university students are offering substantial help is in the area of health care. While most undergraduates are not qualified or licensed to perform medical procedures, they can assist in many ways. In most countries students are allowed to feed, give water to, or bathe patients. Zoology students at American College in Madurai, India, conduct an immunization camp for tribal people while other students organize blood donation camps in the villages. In Ecuador, Universidad San Francisco de Quito's departments of medicine, architecture and environmental studies are responding to the request of an Andean village to build a health clinic.

India

Ecuador

Some universities are encouraging community service by offering such training as paramedical or cardio-pulmonary resuscitation to their student volunteers. Rikkyo University in Tokyo helps its students serve the handicapped more effectively by offering skill-building programs, including reading Braille and speaking sign language.

Japan

Students can and do assist in rehabilitation hospitals, such as the Bernardo's Hospitals in England, guiding the physical exercise of patients under the skilled leadership of a therapist. Or they may help the disabled who live in the community. Also in England, King Alfred's students help those in wheelchairs shop in nearby Winchester. Similarly, at the University of Montpellier in France, students help the disabled move about town. The Hope Valley complex of services to the physically disabled in Jamaica offers an array of placements for students, from teaching in the Experimental School to helping in Monex Industries, a sheltered workshop for the disabled where earphones are sterilized for the airlines and where all Jamaican flags are made.

England

France

Jamaica

Although students may not be allowed to perform technical procedures, they all can provide the needed attention and interest that physicians and nurses know is part of the healing process. In most health-care facilities around the world, the professional staff is stretched to the limit in providing basic medical services. The most caring nurse does not have the luxury of extended visits with patients who may be confined for weeks or even months to their rooms. Eager and cheerful students from Sophia University in Japan tutor bedridden children in local hospitals. St. John's students in Palayamkottai, India, visit the Home for Aged Blind in nearby Tirunelveli, writing letters for the residents to their friends and families, reading, repairing their torn clothes, and acting as companions. Students foster in young and old alike enjoyment of life, sometimes even rekindling in the patient a will to live.

Japan

India

Formerly socialist countries are finding the help of service-learning students critical as they make the transition from government-provided aid to that provided by non-governmental organizations. Charles University's outstanding Faculty of Pedagogy is supplying essential help to the institutions caring for the mentally handicapped in Prague, Czech Republic. This use of students is not confined to one political system or another, for in many capitalist and socialist countries health-care costs have skyrocketed and the effort to contain costs has inevitably meant a reduction in staff.

Czech Republic

Students are also useful in the health-care field by obtaining health information. In agencies serving illiterate clients, students may be assigned the job of interviewing those seeking help and filling out the necessary paperwork for them. Students serve in this capacity in the Bethel comprehensive care center in Jamaica. In Mexico, students gather data from community residents, information used to lobby the government and non-governmental organizations to provide needed health services. Students assist in health care by supporting the distribution of health information and supplies. The French organization Medicine Without Borders utilizes students at the University of Montpellier to repackage drugs donated by French families and companies to send to war-torn areas.

Another major way in which health-care agencies are utilizing students is in teaching about health issues, either directly to community residents or through community health workers. Maternal and prenatal care, nutrition and dental care are taught by students at Trinity College of Quezon City to the residents of the nearby *barangay* (community). Students of Central Philippine University in Iloilo similarly teach about drug addiction, health, sanitation, nutrition, and the prevention of communicable diseases. Students at American College in Madurai, India, teach hygiene and cleanliness as do those from the Universidad Autónoma de Guadalajara, Mexico. In Liberia, Cuttington University students visit villages teaching health awareness and hygiene. College and university students such as those at Isabella Thoburn in Lucknow, India, are effective in teaching about the dangers of drug use and unprotected sexual activity. Supervising physicians report that student health teachers are effective because they bring with them youthful energy, humor, and attractiveness, drawing community residents to participate in the classes they offer.

COMMUNITY DEVELOPMENT

The third area in which students are serving is that of community development. Their help with business enterprises and especially micro-business is one important focus in this area. For example, accounting students at Payap University in Thailand teach their skills to village artisans and entrepreneurs so that they turn a profit sufficient for a living wage. American College students in Madurai, India, teach cottage industries such as matchbox- and candle-making to village women. At Soongsil University in Korea, management and engineering students, working with faculty, offer their specialized knowledge through short-term courses, known as "incubators," for the developers of small businesses. At Trinity College of Quezon City in the Philippines, the biology and business departments have teamed for Project MUSH, teaching local residents to grow mushrooms for freeze-drying and export. Animal husbandry is taught by Cuttington University students to villagers who are then given a pair of pigs or a few chickens. When these animals reproduce, the recipient returns the number of animals he or she first received to the "animal bank" at Cuttington, to be used for further distribution. St. Paul's College in the state of Virginia, the heart of tobacco growing in the United States, has stocked ponds on its large campus with catfish, a popular item on the menus of U.S. restaurants. Because the market for tobacco is diminishing, the college and its students are teaching local small farmers how to switch to catfish farming and harvesting as a means of earning a livelihood. International Christian University in Tokyo and its students have reached beyond national borders by teaching non-chemical farming in its Asian Rural Institute to students from Myanmar, India, Africa, and Pakistan.

Thailand

India

Korea

Philippines

Liberia

United States

Japan

The protection and training of women is a major activity in the area of community development. In addition to helping build micro-businesses and cottage industries, college and university students are serving in programs of nutrition and prenatal care, parenting, day-care centers, and shelters and programs for women who are the victims of family violence. At International University in the Kyrgyz Republic, faculty and students have organized women's groups in the community to promote projects for their advancement. At Sarah Tucker College in Tamil Nadu,

Kyrgyz Republic

India

United States

India, students and faculty help village women bring their grievances to village officials to obtain the services which are their rights by law. St. Augustine College in Chicago, founded in 1980 to serve Hispanic immigrants to the United States, sponsors a day-care center in which mothers study while their children are cared for and taught by service-learning students under direction of professional preschool teachers. The program is bilingual so that Spanish-speaking mothers and children learn English as they simultaneously improve their reading and writing abilities in their native language.

England

Lakota Nation

Another aspect of community development is that of preservation and extension of the cultural heritage. Bishop Grosseteste students in Lincoln, England, perform dramas in hospitals, prisons and schools. On the Lakota Native American tribal reservations in the United States, preservation of the culture is the highest priority. Service-learning students help organize and publicize tribal arts festivals. One was instrumental in founding a now widely-read and respected tribal newspaper. Another catalogued items that had been given to an Indian school over more than a century. The leather, beaded items, and quillwork of this collection are now properly displayed and preserved in a first-rate museum.

India

Indonesia

Philippines

Kodaikanal College in the state of Tamil Nadu, India, has followed the wishes of the nearby tribal peoples in making preservation and teaching of tribal heritage a foundation of their service-learning program. Satya Wacana, in Salatiga, Indonesia, also makes cultural heritage preservation a part of its work in villages. At Trinity College in Quezon City, in the Philippines, one aspect of the college's service is the Samba Likkhan, an artist's colony dedicated to recording and preserving Asian music, especially for those tribes which are diminishing and whose traditional way of life is increasingly difficult to maintain.

Building and maintaining the infrastructure is an important and needed service in many parts of the world. In India, at

American College in Madurai, students lay roads and de-silt tanks. Kattakada College students clean hospitals and construct roads. Plastering, painting, laying foundations, construction—all are included in service-learning around the globe, often in conjunction with Habitat for Humanity (as in Jamaica) or agencies with similar missions. In the United States, students at the distinguished academic institution known as Sewanee, the University of the South, in Tennessee, repair roofs, insulate homes, and chop and deliver firewood for the elderly to prepare them for the cold winters. Service-learning students in Guayaquil, Ecuador, at the Universidad Laica Vicente Rocafuerte; in Jamaica at the University of Technology in Kingston; and in Mexico at the Universidad Autónoma de Guadalajara help design and construct public spaces such as parks, plazas, community centers and playgrounds. In these programs students work alongside the people of the community so that the project meets community needs and esthetic values and will, therefore, be maintained long after the construction is complete and the students have departed.

India

Jamaica
United States

Ecuador
Jamaica

Mexico

Related to community development is environmental protection and education. The marine biology department of Silliman University in Dumaguete, Negros Oriental, in the Philippines, has made a major project of preserving and building colonies of the many varieties of clams once numerous off the coast of the Philippines. Students at Central Philippine University in Iloilo are among the many students around the world who plant trees for their service-learning. Service-learning students at Universidad Espíritu Santo in Guayaquil, Ecuador, work in the ecologically significant dry forest. Trash cleaning is needed all over the world and students are responding. On an appointed day each year, hundreds of students from nearby colleges descend upon the city of Boston, United States, to clean the streets and parks. In Mexico, one service-learning project included teaching children a game that involved picking up trash—a game they enjoyed playing and which still continues long beyond the service of the student. At Bishop Heber College in India,

Philippines

Ecuador

United States
Mexico

India

the environmental studies department conducts study- and teaching-tours to the dense forest and coastal regions. As students and faculty study the ecosystems, they teach environmental preservation and protection to the local people. In *Mexico*, service-learning students, through the local agency El Centro Integral, are teaching the construction of low-cost solar ovens and hot-water systems. In South Dakota, in the United States, a service-learning project videotaped the destruction of a river bank on an Indian reservation as a result of pollutants dumped in the river upstream. The video was used in a lawsuit brought by the Indian tribe against the polluter, helping to win the case.

Mexico

Lakota Nation (U.S.)

Human rights is an issue running throughout many of these service projects. As there are global-scale policy issues related to human rights, so these issues are played out on a local scale, often coming down to specific rights of individuals. In Mexico, service-learning students at Universidad Autónoma de Guadalajara gathered data on a newly developing community, data that were used to convince city officials they needed to provide water, electricity, and schools. Sarah Tucker students in India set up meetings between town officials and members of underserved communities to obtain loans. Service-learning students in Jamaica conducted, under the direction of the Human Rights Council, an extensive study of prison practices for presentations by the HRC to the government. Projects for and with women, indigenous groups, migrants and immigrants almost always involve education about and advocacy for rights. In New York City, service-learners at the largest soup kitchen in the United States, Holy Apostles', are often assigned the job of attending city council meetings to monitor any impending legislation that will affect the plight of the homeless.

Mexico

India

Jamaica

United States

Finally, in all the above-named projects and types of agencies, students may promote the cause by helping in the development of the agency itself. Students gather data, set up computer programs, write brochures and annual reports, fill in government forms, do bookkeeping, compose letters, raise funds, garner community support, and perform myriad other tasks, thereby freeing the professional staff for direct service to the agency's clients.

IN CONCLUSION

In these examples of service—and each example could be duplicated a thousandfold—two patterns are evident. In one, the college faculty and/or students work directly with a village or community group to organize a new project. Examples are programs such as that of Payap University in Thailand; the many village projects in India; those of Satya Wacana and Petra Universities in Indonesia; and the Arab Bedouin project of Ben Gurion University. In this pattern, the university works in partnership with a particular community's leaders—usually a village—to define the needs, plan and execute the project. Often in this pattern, the faculty takes a large part in working with community leaders to design the project. But such is not always the case. In the United States, students at Hobart and William Smith Colleges created and staff an eight-week service- and leadership- program for local thirteen-year-olds. Kenyon College students created a now ten-year-old program serving the people of the Appalachian mountain region, many of whom live in poverty.

Thailand
Indonesia
India
Israel

United States

In the second pattern, students work in an already established agency or project. While the agency may be a government agency or a non-governmental organization (NGO), colleges and universities express preference for the NGOs. The use of NGOs to address community problems is growing around the world. Governments that once created large bureaucracies are cutting budgets for social services and looking to the not-for-profit agencies to pick up the work. Even when government money is available it is being turned over to local and international agencies. These agencies, stretched to the limits of their resources, are welcoming students to assist in addressing a wide variety of needs.

Colleges and universities are joining such international agencies as the World Bank in preferring NGOs. They find them more flexible, less bound by regulations, able to respond quickly, and more attuned to the cultural mores of the community than are government programs and the cumbersome bureaucracies that so often accompany them. This latter pattern is the most common; the agency defines the mission and work and determines the tasks the student will perform. Generally, students fit into an already well-structured program, enriching and adding to the program through their service. Agency personnel supervise the service and the faculty directs reflection and analysis.

Philippines Silliman University in the Philippines is but one of many universities operating service-learning programs in both categories.

Agencies report their preference for service-learning students over volunteers. Agencies that utilize volunteers are disappointed and their programs disrupted by volunteers who drop out when other obligations or enticements come their way. But when the service is a requirement of the university or of the academic studies, students have a high incentive to fulfill the terms of the service. Service-learners typically are reliable and predictable, beginning on a designated day, attending faithfully, and ending their service at the agreed upon time.

A second reason that agency supervisors prefer students is the interest they show in the larger and deeper questions of the work. In many agencies, the supervisor may be the only professionally trained staff member. The students who are interested in the sociology of the clients, the organization of the agency, and its underlying philosophy become, despite their youth and inexperience, like professional colleagues to the supervisor.

Agencies welcome students because they know that university students will become community and national leaders. They know that it is these key people who must be made interested in the problems the agency addresses and who will support their work in the future.

Agencies also tell us that the most helpful service-learning programs are those which allow them, the community organization, to define the work to be done. They believe—correctly—that they know best what their community needs. Community agencies, most of which have operated for years in the community and have staff who come from the community, know well the needs and also know what approaches work and do not work within the cultural context of their community. Universities which insist on defining the project that the students will undertake almost invariably swing wide of the mark, creating additional work for the agency and rendering service that is, in the end, not service at all.

Agency supervisors say as well that they like the fact that the students come as learners, not as outside experts to tell them what they usually already know. One supervisor in a forgotten corner of the world, a U.S. Indian reservation, reports that having students come to learn and serve under their direction is a source of great encouragement to the agency staff. That students, many of whom come from prestigious universities, spend so much time learning from them, is a source of pride and deserved self-esteem.

Lakota Nation (U.S.)

Social problems are growing in communities and nations around the world. There is a well-documented, growing disparity between rich and poor, even in affluent nations and well-established democracies. In some nations, especially of East Africa, the AIDS (SIDA) epidemic is robbing villages of vigorous adults, leaving only the very young and the very old. Even affluent and socially cohesive nations such as Japan are experiencing needs. Rikkyo University, in Tokyo, is establishing a College of Community Welfare Studies. Assistant Director Fumiaki Hasheba has written, "Today Japan is facing a crisis in that there are increasingly small numbers of young people to support increasingly larger numbers of elders."

Japan

The inextricable links between problems and across national

borders requires that the many institutions of society join forces if there is to be any measure of success in addressing these issues. Higher education can and should be a major player. Communities and agencies are welcoming the active participation of college and university students and of their institutions in addressing problems and alleviating suffering.

At the Wingspread Conference, service agency director Victor Maridueña testified to the effect of service-learning:

> To construct the world anew requires a lot of preparation and the removal of some of the debris existing at this moment. We have to remove barriers of prejudice, distrust, resentment, overcautiousness, incredulity, selfishness, complexes, etc. More than a hundred [Partnership] volunteers hosted by Children International - Ecuador have proven that those barriers can be torn down, and for good.
>
> These one hundred young men and women worked directly, sometimes in a one-on-one relationship, with children that could be correctly considered to be "the poorest of the poor." Soon after this encounter, we found that they became one unit of friendship and love, one unit no longer of a first world volunteer and a third world needy child; they became a unit of partners with trust between them, with credulity in their sincerity. They were really the new members of a world anew.

CHAPTER III

PRIMARY MODELS

As colleges and universities seek to link community service to their educational mission they realize that they must design those links to be compatible with their national and institutional cultural context. To be successful they cannot merely replicate the models in use at other institutions. The immediate issues of their communities—the geography, history, mores, and values—must all be part of the way service-learning is organized. So also must the system of education in the nation, the specific mission, structure and regulations of the institution, and the studies of the particular student be taken into account.

First, colleges and universities are, correctly, considering what surrounds and does not surround them. For example, reclamation of the desert is a focus for Ben Gurion University of the Negev in Beer-Sheva, Israel. The Universidad Autónoma de Guadalajara has developed a mobile unit to bring relief to the victims of earthquakes, a recurring problem in Mexico. On the other hand, the University of Aalborg in Denmark is sending its engineering students far afield to Bangladesh, since the affluent, developed and economically homogeneous area of the university provides few opportunities through engineering for service to those in need.

Israel
Mexico

Denmark

Second, service-learning initiators must consider their national system of education. In some places, such as India and Europe, curricula are fixed for an entire course of study of three or four years, especially at public universities. The linking of service with study in fields other than education and social work can be difficult. But determined educators are finding ways around even this structural problem. They are thinking of service-learning not as content but as a pedagogy, thereby enabling the

India
Europe

teacher to fulfill the mandated course requirements but doing so through the techniques of service-learning.

Another way of instituting service-learning in fixed systems of education is for the college or university to require service and the learning derived from it for the diploma, but not to award academic credit. King Alfred's College in Winchester, England, awards a certificate for those completing significant service. Similarly, the University of Montpellier in France has developed a certificate program resulting in a university diploma.

England

France

United States In the United States, by contrast, where each academic institution is largely autonomous and may create its own array of courses, service-learning is easily recognized and credited, provided that the academic work required meets the standards of the college or university. Furthermore, the elective system in which students may study a variety of subjects allows the selection of service-learning for one-fourth or one-fifth of the student's program in any semester. The disadvantage of this system is that the service rendered is limited and the learning derived from it may be superficial since it occupies only a small portion of the student's time and attention.

Third, colleges and universities are designing service-learning based on their own institutional culture—its mission, history and strengths. For example, Lady Doak College, a woman's college founded in 1948 in Madurai, India, has made economic development of village women in the area surrounding the college a prime subject of its service-learning program. Students teach pickling and food preservation, adult literacy, nutrition, AIDS awareness, and the skills of tailoring which help village girls secure employment in the ready-made-garment industries in the area. International Christian University in Tokyo, Japan, honors its founders by sending students to Thailand to work with local congregations to build church buildings.

India

Japan

Finally, colleges and universities consider the course of study of particular students. For example, at the University of New South Wales in Sydney, Australia, students planning careers in medicine serve in the health care sector in indigenous communities.

Australia

Of the many variations on service-learning, five are primary:

CAREER RELATED

In most universities around the world, students enter a course of study with a particular career focus such as business, education, social work, medicine, law, architecture, or engineering. One of these curricula forms the central and in many cases the only academic study for the student in his or her three or four years of university education. These professional tracks have long used the practicum as an important ingredient in career training. At Chung Chi College, one of four divisions of Chinese University of Hong Kong, field service in journalism, education, communications, medicine, and social work is arranged to integrate theory and practice. In Uganda, service-learning is practiced in the field of social work and education at the national university, Makerere, in Kampala, as it is in the other Muslim and Christian universities throughout the nation.

China

Uganda

Now universities are taking up service-learning as a means for students to fulfill practica requirements. At Petra University in Indonesia, students may earn two to three credits in mechanical, civil, electrical, and industrial engineering, architecture, management, accounting, or English for the service they perform. Chester College in England is but one of many British colleges and universities encouraging students to select as their work-based learning requirement a placement with a service agency.

Indonesia

England

Colleges and universities recognize that the line between the traditional practicum and service is a fine one and must be defined within each society, but they are making the distinction between service and the traditional internship in two significant ways.

The first difference is that the service is performed in locations different from the traditional internship. Instead of being in the most prestigious and upper-class schools, practice teaching is carried out in schools for the underprivileged and disadvantaged. Colleges of education are recognizing that success in these schools is a greater measure of the would-be teacher's potential than in schools where by reason of family and school resources pupils already have a distinct advantage in education. Similarly, in business curricula students are being sent to work in micro-business enterprises, in NGOs and in other areas where training workers, managing efficiently, and balancing a budget are more difficult than in already-successful companies.

The second way in which educators around the world are articulating the difference between service-learning and the traditional internship lies in the very purpose and expected outcomes of the practical experience. Traditionally, the focus of an internship has been solely on what the student learned and achieved through the practicum. In service-learning, the focus is shifted to the question of how the community or agency benefited by the student's presence and activity. In service-learning, academic supervisors measure not only what has been learned but also how the recipients of the service have been helped or their lives changed as a result of the student's work.

DISCIPLINE RELATED

Many university systems around the world require the liberal arts student to declare his or her focus upon entering in a way similar to that of the career-track studies. In the disciplines of the natural sciences, especially in biology and environmental studies, and in some disciplines of the social sciences, especially political science, sociology, archaeology, ethnography, and anthropology, field study has long been incorporated into the course of the academic work. In these fields direct observation lies at the very heart of the methodology by which knowledge is acquired. Field study is also sometimes incorporated in the humanities in disciplines such as linguistics and language study, literature, philosophy, religion, and the arts.

Now teachers are introducing service-learning as an important and clearly distinct method of learning the skills of these disciplines. For example, Trinity College of Quezon City, in the Philippines, includes students of arts and sciences, global studies and psychology in its service-learning programs. In the United States, Hobart/William Smith Colleges offer twenty different service-learning courses (modules) in the disciplines of political science, education, sociology, religious studies, chemistry, rhetoric, philosophy, economics, African studies, and Latin American studies.

Philippines

United States

The department of zoology at American College in Madurai, India, has a decade-old program through which they have now immunized more than four hundred tribal children against the diseases of polio, diphtheria, whooping cough and tetanus, educated hundreds of adults about health issues and extended to them basic health care for such illnesses as respiratory track infection, arthritis, severe anemia, worm infection, fever, vitamin deficiency, gastroenteritis, and bronchitis.

India

Under the direction of Dr. R. Dinakaran Michael, head of the postgraduate and research department of zoology, the program began with male undergraduate students and later was expanded to include women and graduate students. Involving women increased the access to village women; the graduates brought a higher level of skills to the work. The program, involving about one hundred and fifty students, operates with a team of six or eight students and one medical doctor who is usually an alumnus of the zoology department of the college and who donates his or her services. Beginning early on a Saturday morning, the college van takes the team to a village, allowing three or four mountain villages to be covered in a day. Students use the skills learned in biology class to analyze blood and urine samples, and in recording blood pressure and other medical information.

Although it is impossible within the scope of this study to estimate the extent of change in these various disciplines, there does appear to be a new mindset with regard to field study. Anthropologists, ethnographers, and sociologists are voicing two important shifts. They have long recognized that the very presence of an observer changes the behavior of the community being observed. Now they are acknowledging that the student who is only an observer is often denied access to information, whether deliberately or unconsciously, by the community. The service-learner, on the other hand, becomes a working member of the community. Trust is inspired by the contribution he or she is making, thereby opening doors to case histories of agency clients and internal workings of the service organization.

A second reason researchers give for valuing and promoting service-learning as opposed to traditional observation is the recognition that fieldwork can be and often is exploitative of the community being studied. Academics studying a particular community must ask local people for their time and resources. The researcher returns to his or her institution to write books and thereby earn career promotions as a result of his or her study without any real benefit accruing to those who have cooperated in the study. However, most academics care—or come to care—about the people whose environment and communities they study. When they and their students contribute through service in practical and real ways to the community as they learn from it, they are to some extent balancing the relationship and the interaction.

COURSE/MODULE RELATED

United States In the United States or in U.S.-based systems of education, the individual course (called in the U.S. a "course," in Britain, a "module") makes up a small percentage of the student's four-year degree program. In these systems, the primary model for linking service and learning is that of tying the service to one of these courses. The student may be majoring in any one of a wide variety of disciplines and preparing for any one of many careers, yet may study as one-fourth or one-fifth of his or her studies in any given semester a subject in which service is a co-requisite. Students may, for example, study homelessness in America and simultaneously be required to perform service in a shelter for the homeless. While the service is not very intense—usually only one to four hours a week for twelve weeks—such courses are a means of introducing many students to community problems and to the experience of service.

Within this model are two important variations:

<u>Single Course/Existing Disciplines</u>

Widespread is the use of a single, existing course coming from an established discipline or academic department. The most common form of this is found in human services and social sciences, particularly sociology and psychology. But increasingly, faculty in such disciplines as economics, environmental science, political science, literature, philosophy, and religion are re-describing their existing courses to include the experience of service as one of the requirements for fulfilling the academic assignments and mastering the subject of the study.

In this model, service may be assigned to all members of a class or may be an optional addition to traditional classroom-based study. By performing service and writing a paper analyzing the issues and experiences in the agency, students selecting this option often earn additional academic credit. Among the U.S. colleges offering such an options are the University of South Carolina, Florida State University, and Bates College in Maine.

<u>Single Course/Created Study</u>

A growing number of colleges and universities are developing studies particularly designed for the service experience. These may be related closely to existing and accepted disciplines, or involve multi- or inter-disciplinary content and methodologies. They may be rooted in a particular academic department or may be inter-departmental. Examples may also be found based in student services, freshman orientation programs, senior seminars, or counseling offices. At St. Augustine's College in Raleigh, North Carolina, in the United States, a service-learning course includes issues of business and professional behavior. Topics for class study and discussion include workplace preparedness, time management, public speaking and effective communication, leadership skills, and behavior in the service agency. "Volunteer: Theory and Practice" is the title of the service-learning course at Sophia University in Tokyo, Japan. The student, in consultation with the professor offering the course, develops a plan for service and learning, and then records daily activities and reflections. The professor and student meet periodically to monitor and evaluate the progress. At Soongsil University, in Korea, a two-credit social service course is offered during vacation periods. Under the supervision of the accompanying professor, students may select a nine-day service experience in the Philippines or Nepal or they may choose a three-week rural or urban service in Korea. University (of Leeds) College of Ripon and York, in England, has created a course entitled "Understanding Organizations," which focuses on personal and professional development to give the student knowledge and understanding of himself or herself and of work environments from which comes a career development plan.

United States

Japan

Korea

England

THE COHESIVE CURRICULUM

One of the most intense, sophisticated, and interesting models is that in which two or more disciplines or professional tracks are brought together around a service opportunity. Requiring a team of teachers from different fields, these service-learning programs demonstrate collaborative teaching and learning and the need for a coordinated approach to problems.

In some of these programs, a particular student may be using a single service experience to study more than one subject or discipline. Programs of The International Partnership for Service-Learning are so organized. Students serve in their placement approximately eighteen hours a week for a semester, year or summer, and simultaneously study such subjects as sociology, history, political science, language, literature, economics, anthropology, religion, education, ethnography, and various cultural studies. The academic work covers major concepts of the discipline and utilizes the student's experience in the agency as one valuable resource along with reading, lectures, research, and other traditional academic tools for understanding the material at hand.

In another variation of the cohesive curriculum, the service may be a group project with students in the group approaching the learning and service from several different disciplines or career training tracks. In this model they share their varying approaches through the work they are doing together.

For example, Dr. Aris Pongtuluran, Rector of Petra University in Surabaya, Indonesia, explained that groups of their students and faculty work with single villages whose residents define the service they wish to have performed:

Indonesia

> The majority of people in Indonesia live in the suburbs and the condition of the villages is still far behind....To support their development, Petra University uses education and research, applying technology and friendly environmental systems which are acceptable to the society and will improve the people's welfare. It is part of Petra's threefold responsibilities: teaching, research and community service. Called *Kuliah Kerja Nyata*, the service is designed to ensure that students put all their theoretical knowledge into practice. In the first stage, they conduct research on the real problems faced by the village. They then formulate a program that will empower the local people with the skills to enhance their welfare. They dig out the potential of the village. In the program the students are trained to work across sectors of the society and utilize many disciplines, enabling them to work in the real field that is different from the major they are studying. At the end of the program, the

students write an evaluation on which the next phase of the program is based, a phase to be carried out by the succeeding students.

Ecuador In Ecuador, the faculty and students of the Universidad San Francisco de Quito, studying medicine, the environment, and architecture, work with Andean towns to establish health clinics that will provide health services in settings compatible with the traditions and environmental conditions of the community.

Philippines At Trinity College of Quezon City in the Philippines, the business and biology departments have teamed up on a project that teaches the useful job skills of mushroom growing, harvesting, and marketing to residents of the nearby squatters' community. Biology students help the budding entrepreneurs plant the mushroom spores on logs used as the growing medium. They then teach how to care for the mushroom colony and when to harvest. The business department provides the space where the mushrooms are freeze-dried and packaged, and business students teach the skills of pricing and marketing.

The advantages of this model are evident in the quality of both the service and the learning. From the service perspective, the advantage of the cohesive curriculum model lies in the amount of time students are able to spend in the service. This enables the agency to use the student to the fullest, giving him or her more responsibility than can be assigned to those who only spend a few short hours in service, with consequent benefits to the service agency. With regard to the learning, this model fosters in students both deeper and broader learning, demonstrating that academic disciplines are but a means of seeing, ordering, and understanding a complex world. The learning is collaborative and active. And because of the position and responsibilities the student is given in the agency, he or she learns more about the workings of the organization or village, practices intensely the required behavior, and emerges with enhanced skills—and an enhanced resume.

NON-CREDITED BUT PART OF THE LEARNING EXPECTATIONS

Volunteer service as an extra-curricular activity has, of course, long been a part of the life of many universities and colleges around the world. Of special note are those institutions which have such a strong system of values that students enter with the expectation that acquiring these values will be as much a part of their learning as will formal, classroom and credited learning.

Lady Doak College in India is one such college. Young women select Lady Doak because they know that since its founding it has been committed to women's leadership and development. They know of the graduates who have gone forth to high positions and they expect to learn the skills that will allow them to do likewise. The service projects with village women are part of this training for Lady Doak students. Although not credited in academic studies, students participate for the learning they know they want to and will acquire. *India*

Another example of strong and definable college values is that of the United States Naval Academy. Like Lady Doak students, aspirants hope to gain admission to the Academy not only for the fine academic education it provides, but equally for the qualities of discipline, leadership, courage, loyalty, and honor that are thought to characterize its graduates. Midshipmen who partake in the "Mids and Kids" service project tutor local children. In doing so they are conscious that through their service they are acting as role models for the children and simultaneously reinforcing in themselves the qualities they came to the Naval Academy to acquire. *United States*

Service in institutions strongly identified with a clear mission and set of values is recognized as integral to its teaching and learning whether or not it is credited.

IN CONCLUSION

The growth of service-learning around the world and the models on which it is based vary according to the conditions and values of the community and of the particular institution and course of study. Just as the reasons educators give for developing service-learning are not based on imitation of an admired system of education in another nation, and as the service rendered answers the needs of a specific community, so the models that are being developed spring from the particular circumstances of each society and system of education. While educators welcome ideas from other institutions and nations, they adapt the general concept of service-learning to their particular situation.

Many institutions of higher education around the world are seeking to define their specific goals and give concrete expression to the rhetoric of mission statements and convocation and commencement addresses. They seem to be unwilling to imitate uncritically other recognizably successful universities, but rather carve out their special area for excellence and contribution. Smaller institutions especially, which acknowledge that they cannot compete in the arena of research, are seeing community service as a means of defining who they are. They are working hard at creating a strong tradition of values that will make them appealing to applicants and their parents and help institutions gain the approval and support of the communities in which they are located and on which they depend.

All of this is an encouraging sign for the future of service-learning because the success of service-learning depends on its compatibility with the values and systems in which it must reside.

CHAPTER IV

RELATED ISSUES

Following the decision of which model will be used to link learning to service are a series of correlative issues. Ideally, the academic institution and the service agencies and community leaders decide together how to pattern the service-learning program.

GROUP OR INDIVIDUAL STUDY AND SERVICE

A key question for program designers is whether the study and service will be organized for a group of students or individualized for a particular student. There are four possible patterns.

Group Study, Group Service

In this pattern students engage in the same set of studies and perform the same type of service. The service may be at the same agency or in separate but similar agencies. This is the most frequently used design, as in the case of education students conducting their practice teaching in schools or environmental studies students working together to plant trees.

Group Study, Individual Service

Here students are engaged in the same set of studies but are performing different types of service. The service is usually carried out in different agencies, but it may be within the same agency if the agency is large, has a variety of objectives and activities, and is so organized to utilize the services of a number of students. Ewha University in Korea, the largest women's university in the world, has such a program. Together students are prepared for service through common study and then are stationed in many different agencies providing a wide range of services. The general organization of the programs of The

Korea

International Partnership for Service-Learning follows this pattern. All students take a six-credit course (a double module), entitled "Institutions in Society," dealing with the major cultural patterns of the society. Each student is then assigned placement in an agency according to the student's interests and skills. In class, the students analyze their various agencies, seeing them as a kind of microcosm of the issues facing the larger society.

Individual Study, Group Service

India

Students may be engaged in the same service project but are using the experience to study different subjects. For example, St. John's College in Palayamkottai, India, in a project funded by the Ford Foundation, adopted Tharuvai, a village of fifteen hundred people a few miles from the college campus. Under the banner of a "Campus Diversity Initiative," the students from various disciplines and professional training programs offered legal advice and taught "awareness" classes dealing with AIDS, polio prevention, and career guidance for youth. They organized medical camps, sports matches and debates on important issues, or planted trees, according to their field of study. Payap University in Chiang Mai, Thailand, is expecting to initiate such a system of service-learning. Using the provision in the curriculum for "Independent Studies," Payap students engaged in the large and active volunteer service program of the university will be able to engage in group work with other student volunteers, yet attach academic learning to their service and thus receive academic recognition.

Thailand

Individual Study, Individual Service

Japan

Here the student and teacher decide the learning goals and methods and the student performs the related service in an agency chosen by the college or, more frequently, selected by the student. At Sophia University in Japan, students in the course entitled "Volunteer: Theory and Practice" draw up their own plan of service and study under the guidance of an advisor.

CONCURRENT, ALTERNATING OR SEQUENCED LEARNING AND SERVICE

A second issue of program design is the sequencing of the service and the learning. Decisions may hinge on geographic location of the campus and the service(s) to be performed, and on the calendar and daily schedule of the university and of the agencies.

<u>Concurrent Study and Service</u>

The student attends regularly scheduled classes several days a week and performs the service at some time during the same weeks. This is a frequent pattern in locations such as cities where the service to be performed is geographically near the place of study. It also works well when the activities of the agency are ongoing or follow the same calendar as the academic institution. Ideal is the situation in which academic classes and the activities of the agency are scheduled for different times of day. For example, in universities whose classes are mainly in late afternoon or evening, service in school programs for young children work well. When college classes are scheduled for mornings, after-school programs serving children become a convenient way to serve.

<u>Sequenced Learning and Service</u>

Instead of occurring concurrently, the service and learning may be organized sequentially. In some locations, such as the Philippines, this is called "block placement." The most frequent variation is a period of preparation followed by a period of service. Less frequently the service is followed by a period of reflection. *Philippines*

In Ecuador at Universidad San Francisco de Quito, students take a preparation seminar and, when completed, begin work in the service agency. The same is true of the program at Ewha University in Korea. University of Technology students in *Ecuador*

Korea

Jamaica Jamaica follow their service with a comprehensive report, describing the outcomes of their service.

Alternating Learning and Service

A third pattern is that of alternating the study and the service, most frequently a period of preparation followed by a period of service and concluding with a period of reflection on what has been learned and accomplished. In the final period, the academic work related to the service—papers, presentations, and examinations—is concluded.

The multidisciplinary village development projects of Satya Wacana in Salatiga, Indonesia, conform to this plan, with the notable feature being that village leaders as well as faculty and students participate during the preparation period in defining and planning the project to be carried out. After the preparation, which occurs both on campus and in the field, the students and faculty move to the village to carry out the work in collaboration with the villagers. In the last stage, students prepare a written report, evaluating the progress to date and making recommendations for the next team to take up the project.

REQUIRED OR OPTIONAL SERVICE-LEARNING

A major decision to be made by a college or university is whether to require that students complete a service assignment at some time in their higher education or whether to make service optional. Of course, most institutions choose the latter, and those that do require service of their students began by developing a strong optional service program. Required service may by an institutional requirement of all students, or a requirement within a department. When tied to academic learning, the student is generally awarded academic credit.

Another pattern is that the service is not recognized for academic credit but is required for graduation. A surprising number of colleges and universities around the world require a period of volunteer service for graduation. Two universities in Ecuador—Universidad Espíritu Santo and Universidad San Francisco de Quito—require students to complete a period of service prior to graduation. The University of Technology in Kingston, Jamaica, makes a similar demand. Cuttington University in Liberia requires all students to study rural development and perform a related service. Sungkonghoe University is one of the Korean institutions of higher education with a service graduation requirement. In the United States, the primary national service-learning organization, Campus Compact, conducted a survey of its membership of colleges and universities. Of the 266 institutions returning the survey, 8.3 percent indicated that they require students to be engaged in service sometime in their four years in order to graduate.

Ecuador

Jamaica
Liberia

Korea
United States

Many more examples exist, from virtually all countries surveyed, in which service is a requirement within a department or a particular curriculum of a university. In Uganda, for example, university departments in social work, health care, child care, and counseling require a service experience.

Uganda

YEAR-SPECIFIC OR ONGOING

Most colleges and universities with service and service-learning programs make the opportunities ongoing, permitting the students to take part at any time in their education.

At some colleges and universities, service-learning is designed for and sometimes required of students during a specific year of study, such as the first or fourth year.

At Sungkonghoe University in Seoul, Korea, all students must perform thirty hours of volunteer service in their freshman year. Called "*sawhebongsa*" or "volunteer service for society," the service and study is supervised by faculty in the department of social welfare. Voorhees College in the United States has a

Korea

United States

Jamaica

England

similar requirement for service during the freshman year. The University of Technology in Kingston, Jamaica, requires first-year service which, if not completed, increases in subsequent years. In England, at Christ Church College in Canterbury, a division of the University of Kent, students must complete a work placement in their second year. Service in community agencies, an option for the work placement, is chosen by many students.

Japan

At Rikkyo University in Tokyo, the College of Community Welfare has a sequenced program throughout the four years. As freshmen, the students create a human interview document and then interview someone in a social-welfare institution, reporting on their life and the challenges they face in their work. In their second year, students conduct field studies; in the third year they volunteer in agencies—at home or overseas. The fourth year is spent in preparing for the licensing procedure.

LOCAL, OFF-CAMPUS OR INTERNATIONAL

Service-learning may be designed and approved for study at the home university with service performed in the local community. This is, of course, by far the most common pattern, one that could be available to virtually all students around the world, for there is no community, however small, which has no needs for students to fill. Even in the most rural campus settings, faculty with imagination are finding ways for the students to learn and serve.

Indonesia

India

Another pattern frequently employed is that of service away from the campus community but supervised by faculty from the sponsoring institution. The faculty may or may not accompany the students. The many village programs in Indonesia and India are examples of this pattern. The distinguished St. John's College in Agra, India, organized about fifteen colleges from various states of India for service projects of twenty days. The students came from a cross-section of India's geographic and religious diversity, thus reinforcing one of the outcomes of service-learning as providing cross-cultural experiences. For this service the program officer and one student participant were awarded the prestigious Indira Gandhi National Award.

The service may be in the home nation or it may be in another nation with accompanying faculty from the home institutions. Aalborg University students from Denmark have university-sponsored projects in Bangladesh. Ewha University in Korea sends students each year for service in Nepal, China, Bangladesh, and Russia. King Alfred College students in England serve in sub-Saharan Africa and in India.

Denmark

Korea

England

Another possibility for service-learning off campus is for the home institution to accept transfer credit for the student who goes off campus or to another nation to study as well as serve. Academic work is conducted by the institution at the place of service. This is the pattern for colleges and universities participating in programs of The International Partnership for Service-Learning. Each year, students from about twenty countries leave their home college or university for a summer, semester or year to participate in a Partnership program combining substantive volunteer service with rigorous academic study in one of twelve nations around the world. In cooperation with an affiliated university in the location of the program, the Partnership arranges service placements, academic instruction, housing, orientation, field trips, and other support services. At the end of the program an official grade report is sent by the affiliated university to the Partnership for each student. These are then forwarded to the student's home institution for recording.

INTENSITY OF LEARNING AND SERVICE

Service–learning programs vary in the duration and intensity of the service and the depth and extent of the learning. In some programs, the service required may be very little—for example,

India

Canada

Korea

a total of eight or ten hours. Or the service may require a deep commitment of time. Students at St. John's College in Agra give an average of 252 hours per year. The service-learning students at Renison College at the University of Waterloo, Canada, put in four hundred hours of service which is supervised and evaluated by the faculty in Social Development studies. Soongsil University management and engineering students in Korea spend a hundred and twenty to a hundred and fifty hours per year in their service assignment.

In some programs, the students may be credited or the service may be otherwise recognized with very little evidence required for the learning. The keeping of a journal or verbal reporting is not unusual in programs which recognize the service in some way on the student's record but do not award academic credit.

India

This is a common pattern in colleges and universities in India where no formal academic credit is given but which require participation in co-curricular activities. Service thus given weight becomes very important when a student applies for a new course of study, such as graduate school.

In other programs, the academic learning may be demanding and rigorous, requiring class attendance, library research, case studies, substantial papers, presentations, interviews, and examinations. The International Partnership for Service-Learning, for example, is clear that academic credit is awarded for academic work only, not for the service in and of itself. The service experience is but one means along with traditional methods for learning such as reading, writing, and attending lectures, and it is the demonstrated learning which is credited.

IN CONCLUSION

Just as there are many academic studies that are being linked to service and many types of service being performed by service-learning students, so there are many patterns of program organization. Of the choices outlined above, many combinations are possible. There are advantages and disadvantages to each and the designers of programs need to be aware of them. For example, group service/group study is the most cost-efficient and easily managed. It has the additional advantage of allowing the students to serve cooperatively on a project, learning the skills of collaboration. Individual placement, on the other hand, fosters responsibility and independence in a very special way, as students individually placed in agencies are considered to be a staff member and almost always assume the behavior of mature adults in performing their duties.

To win approval of the academic institution, service-learning must fit the system and standards of the institution. Service-learning programs which award the student academic credit without the rigor demanded in regular university classes will never be honored by the majority of the faculty and may, as a result, be short-lived. Fortunately, most students respond well to demanding programs and thus the fear of failure to recruit students may be allayed.

To achieve ongoing support and cooperation from communities and agencies, university service-learning programs must offer them real help. Agencies drop out of programs when programs demand too much supervising, reporting, and paper work from the already over-worked staff; when the students give too little time to be useful; when the academic institution tries to dictate to the agency a service project which may not fit its needs or priorities; when students are unwilling or unaware that they must take direction from the staff and abide by the policies and cultural norms of the agency; and when the agency is not compensated for financial outlay related to the student's service. But it is a truth universally acknowledged that when these matters are properly arranged, the agencies are generous with their supervisory time and welcoming of the students.

To interest students and earn their commitment, service-learning programs must fit the level of skills and maturity of the student. Students wish to be challenged appropriately and welcome the opportunity to be truly useful. They are disappointed, disillusioned, and frustrated when the service they are asked to do is too little or is poorly organized so that in the end they feel that they have wasted their time. Conversely, if the agency expects too much—for example in expressing disappointment that they are not trained professionals—then they are discouraged from future service.

Getting it right requires ongoing communication and cooperation between the academic institution and the agency. Educators must heed the plea of agency personnel that service-learning not be entered into unless there is agreement to a long-term commitment. The up-front time required for designing a program and for the agency and university to get acquainted is too great to invest for a program that will be offered only once or twice. Mistakes often occur in the first efforts, both on the part of the university and of the agency. Fine-tuning takes time.

University faculty and administrators, agency supervisors, and students agree that this investment is well worth the effort. A good program in the end provides much help to communities, proves to be a powerful educational experience for the students, is enlivening for faculty, returns the institution to its high purpose, and establishes good relations within communities.

CHAPTER V

INSTITUTIONAL COMMITMENT

The president of a university in Poland is reported to have commented, "While we have some public-service activities at our universities, we have never institutionalized the concept. Our challenge is to integrate it into the fabric of the institution."[7] His situation is shared by many institutional heads around the world, for in most institutions, service-learning is occurring in only a few departments of the university. These departments struggle to gain recognition and win support from the university as a whole that does not, as yet, realize the enriching impact service-learning can have on all students in all disciplines. What else these universities might not perceive is that the institutionalization of service-learning assists in developing a cohesive curriculum for students, enabling them to understand different disciplines in relation to one another and to society.

Poland

Yet there are notable examples of institutions that do realize the potential of service-learning and have therefore developed an institution-wide commitment. It is in these institutions that the effects of service-learning are likely to be greatest. The values embodied in service-learning and the education reform implied is perceived as lying at the very heart of these universities' missions. They understand that the greatest impact on the development of the service ethic in students will come when the university itself demonstrates strongly and visibly its commitment to service in the community, the nation, and the world.

When institutional resources are pledged by the board of

---

7. From *Carpathia Project Report: Building Bridges Between Institutions of Higher Education in the Carpathian Region of East Central Europe and the Southeastern United States: First Phase Report*. From the Associated Colleges of the South, sponsored with USAID.

governors or trustees; when the college or university head speaks and supports service projects through policy; when the communities served are full participants; and when faculty and students are engaged in the service-learning activities of their institution, then true educational reform takes place and the values enumerated in Chapter I become a way of life.

ENTRY POINTS

The institutionalization of service-learning can occur in a variety of ways; each institution must identify for itself the steps it needs to take to bring service-learning to the forefront. By studying the development of service-learning at colleges and universities that have made a strong institutional commitment, it is possible to identify four main entry points. Each entry point can be seen as an example of leadership since service-learning is only institutionalized with the assistance of a strong leader or leaders.

The first entry point is leadership from the rector, president, or principal. At these institutions, the first person to address and provide support for service-learning is the head, who convenes meetings of the board of trustees or governors and the faculty to discuss the importance of such an endeavor. Heads who take the lead in service-learning are willing to use their university's resources to support community service projects, linking them with educational goals of the university. Where service-learning is led from the top, faculty members are likely to be rewarded for their work in service-learning. From this entry point, the connection of service-learning to every aspect of the institution will be accomplished in the least amount of time.

The second entry point leading to the institutionalization of service-learning is faculty leadership. In this model, one faculty member, or an entire department, supports service-learning and introduces it within his or her discipline. But to lead to university-wide commitment, one member of this group must take on the role of a mentor for faculty from other disciplines. The more respected and senior the service-learning mentor, the more quickly the pedagogy will expand from discipline to discipline. While this path may take more time than the first, it can lead to the institutionalization of service-learning if the faculty as a whole approves it, recognizes its merits, and supports faculty members who use it.

A third entry point is that of student leadership. Around the world, students at universities are participating in service projects that are not connected to their academic studies. There are students who realize the learning potential of service and express, often with great passion, their beliefs to the faculty and/or the college head. Students can effectively act as advocates, interesting their faculty in connecting service to their courses. At some institutions, students play a more sophisticated role in service-learning by acting as liaisons with local agencies.

A fourth entry point may be an outside organization. In the United States, Campus Compact has brought visibility and taught technique to campuses across the country. Colleges and Universities of the Anglican Communion and the United Board for Christian Higher Education in Asia have sponsored programs in cooperation with The International Partnership for Service-Learning which have brought students from many nations to learn and serve together. The power of these experiences has been reported by the students to their own institutions, which in turn have developed local programs. Funding organizations such as private foundations and trusts, including the Ford Foundation and British Petroleum, have inspired colleges and universities to become involved in service-learning. Similarly, government sponsored programs such as the National Community Service Act in the United States and the National Service Schemes in India and Israel have been entry points for the institutionalization of service-learning.

United States

India
Israel

An important early step in institutionalizing service-learning programs is that of connecting it to the institution's mission. Most universities list outreach as part of their mission, but few enumerate concrete programmatic expressions of this element. Those initiating service-learning on a campus make clear the link between service-learning and the institution's mission, thus encouraging greater support from all members of campus and lending support for the case that service-learning is an essential part of education and not merely peripheral. When this is done, the governing board generally joins enthusiastically in supporting service-learning.

As the commitment to service-learning grows on a campus, a university-wide service-learning committee is formed. Regardless of which of the four points becomes the entry for service-learning, successful programs thrive when a diverse group of faculty, students, staff, and community members work together to generate support and promote service-learning university-wide. When led by a senior administrator who has been appointed by the head, the committee will help to alleviate any fragmentation. It promotes the movement of service-learning from one department or one person's hands to the entire university and ensures that when leadership changes for any reason, the programs of service-learning and the advocacy of connections between the university and the needs of its community, nation and the world will continue. Realizing the importance of the university-wide committee, The International Partnership for Service-Learning has instituted a program naming selected institutions as "Distinguished Partners," inviting their university committee to form a chapter of IPS-L and award to their students the Distinguished Service-Learning Award. (Details of this program are contained in Appendix 4).

The institutional commitments of six very different colleges and universities illustrate several possible approaches:

CUTTINGTON UNIVERSITY COLLEGE, SUACOCO, LIBERIA

No university offers a more dramatic example of the need for and benefits of service-learning than Cuttington University College. Founded in 1889, Cuttington is the oldest private co-educational four-year degree-granting institution in sub-Saharan Africa. Known as "the Harvard of West Africa," Cuttington has sent its graduates around the world into positions of leadership in government, business, and other prestigious professions. At least fifty percent of junior ministers and sixty percent of medical doctors in Liberia during the previous administration were Cuttington graduates.

But in May, 1990, the learning and teaching at Cuttington came to a halt as rebel soldiers advanced toward the campus. One year earlier, civil unrest had begun in Liberia, with the goal of toppling the dictatorial regime. With the takeover of the campus by rebel troops, the college was formally closed and faculty and staff fled for their lives. Realizing that with each passing month the college was closed it would become more difficult to reopen, the president, Dr. Melvin Mason, himself a Liberian and a graduate of Cuttington, developed with colleagues a plan for Cuttington University-in-Exile. A board was established and offices were offered by St. Paul's College in Lawrenceville, Virginia, in the United States. Throughout the civil war, Cuttington-in-Exile placed refugee students in colleges and universities around the world, helped its faculty use the time for additional study; and worked to build a constituency of supporters who would aid in rebuilding when the time was right.

Finally, peace was achieved and it became possible to reopen the college in 1998. By the end of the war, Dr. Mason had developed a plan for the new Cuttington. The plan built on the former reputation of Cuttington for academic excellence, but called for a new modus operandi. The devastated nation needed massive rebuilding and Cuttington faculty and students would need to put their shoulders to the wheel.

Liberia

Now, after ten years, the campus has reopened, and Cuttington is once again a place of learning and teaching. But now it is also a place of outreach to the community. During the ten years of civil war, most Liberians did not attend school, creating a dramatic need for remedial education. Also, farming and animal husbandry skills needed to be taught and mastered once again. Therefore, Dr. Mason's plan for the reopened Cuttington has service-learning at its center, with three foci: health care, literacy, and economic development. Students and faculty visit towns and villages near the university to educate residents on public and community health practices in order to minimize illness. Medicine is to be brought to the sick through community clinics supervised by the college nursing division, precisely the type of hands-on experience future doctors and nurses need in order to fully understand their studies.

Education students as well as students from other majors are involved in improving the literacy of surrounding communities. They teach in village schools, helping children learn the basics of reading and writing. But they are not only helping children. The war created a generation of undereducated people; many of traditional college age also need remedial education. Cuttington is offering basic literacy and numeracy courses for these individuals.

One of the most important aspects of Cuttington's service-learning program is the focus on rural development. All students entering Cuttington must take one year of rural development, during which they are required to master the basics of animal husbandry, vegetable farming, water sanitation, and other such essentials. Students work with local villagers, teaching the skills they have just learned. One specific example is the establishment of pig farms in three villages. Students and faculty work with these villages, teaching them how to raise pigs. The eventual goal is that offspring from the pigs, as well as the knowledge of caring for them, will be passed from village to village, making the villagers self-sufficient. The animal bank maintained on campus gives villagers who have been so trained a pair of piglets or a few chickens. When these reproduce, the villager returns the number he or she was given and thus the stock in the bank remains.

Cuttington perceives that its role in society must be as a leader in the rebuilding of the nation. The mission of the reopened Cuttington is to teach not only the students who enter the campus but also the people of Liberia. The university is using its now meager resources to connect the learning on campus with the development of the nation.

TRINITY COLLEGE, CONNECTICUT, UNITED STATES

Another college which has institutionalized service-learning is Trinity College of Hartford, Connecticut, in the United States. Founded in 1823, Trinity is among America's most prestigious private colleges and has recently become known for its commitment to the local community.

United States

Across the street from Trinity College is one of America's most troubled neighborhoods, the Frog Hollow/Barry Square Community. The impoverished area was filled with drugs, and many residents were uneducated and educational resources were sparse. Little was being done to improve the situation until 1995, when the new president of Trinity, Dr. Evan Dobelle, decided that the college had a duty to help improve the neighborhood. "It would be morally bankrupt to teach the liberal arts on our campus and ignore what is happening across the street," he stated. Thus began the Trinity College commitment to and connection with its neighboring community.

Today Trinity has invested approximately $6 million of its own money in the community and has leveraged over $175 million in support from various companies, foundations, and the local government. The goal is to work with the community to develop a "safe, viable, neighborhood which is also a central hub of educational, health and family support and economic development activities." In order to accomplish this, Trinity is working with community organizations already in existence.

The first area of development is called the Learning Corridor. This is an area of the community which will contain a number of schools and training centers. The local Montessori Elementary will relocate to this corridor and expand to hold more students. A new Hartford Public Middle School will be built within the corridor, as will a high school resource center that will improve the education of students from the Hartford area. Educators will have the chance to improve their skills through a new teacher training center.

Trinity is going beyond education, however, as it continues to work with the local community. The college was instrumental in developing the HART Jobs Center/Centro Comunal de Trabajos, an employment resource organization. Local residents, including many Latino immigrants, can find training and employment opportunities through this organization. In addition to helping people find jobs, Trinity and the local community are working to create home ownership opportunities for residents; few homes in the selected areas are owner-occupied.

Two other areas of focus will help improve the neighborhood: a Boys and Girls Club and a Center for Families. Trinity's Boys and Girls Club is the first to be opened at a college or university. The club, dedicated to promoting the character, health and career aspirations of children ages six to thirteen who lack access to constructive opportunities, will be partially staffed by Trinity students who are positive role models for the preteen children. The Center for Families will work with very young children, helping them prepare for school, as well as provide classes on parent education and wellness to their parents. In addition, it will offer a day-care center for the children of local families.

Trinity's entire plan connects directly to the academic courses and learning taking place on campus. President Dobelle expects every student to serve in the local community in one of the twenty-five projects that have been developed or expanded. Classes on campus explore larger issues but ground them through studies of the local community. As in other service-learning programs, students engaged in these classes gain a deeper understanding of issues in the community, laying the groundwork for service it is hoped they will perform once they have graduated and are in leadership positions.

UNIVERSIDAD AUTONOMA DE GUADALAJARA (UAG), MEXICO

The first private university in Mexico, Universidad Autónoma de Guadalajara was born out of the political controversies in Mexico in the 1930s. The public university of Guadalajara, the second largest city in Mexico, had become heavily communist. After student unrest resulted in riots, a group of dissatisfied professors and students withdrew and founded UAG. "They felt the need to become defenders of the freedom of thought threatened by attempts to base higher education on doctrines of a dogmatic and totalitarian nature, alien to the feeling of our people and to the tenets expressed in Mexico's Political Constitution of 1917."[9]

Mexico

One of the young students who were part of the founding of Autónoma, as it is known to the people of the city, was Dr. Luis Garibay, later to become the rector of the university, and who led it to become a university of world renown. Today the university enrolls 21,000 students in its over sixty-four undergraduate and graduate programs. Students come from all over Latin America, as well as the United States, Canada, Europe, and Asia to study medicine, law, education, the arts and humanities, ar-

---

9. *The Universidad Autónoma de Guadalajara and its Faithful Commitment to Mexican Society*, published by UAG.

chitecture, engineering, social work, business and an array of other subjects. Its faculty members publish widely the results of their first-rate research. In 1996, Autónoma built the first community college of Mexico, UNICO. Under Dr. Garibay's leadership, Autónoma became an early and primary promoter of international education, and for many years it was the location of the general secretariat of the International Association of University Presidents.

From its earliest days, the leaders of Autónoma were concerned about the welfare of the people of Mexico and especially of the state of Jalisco, of which Guadalajara is the capital. Dr. Garibay and colleagues believed that those with the privilege of education ought to use it for the good of others. The medical school of the university, which was to achieve great distinction, pioneered the idea of students serving in the community. The University established clinics, "Intecos," throughout the city, where the poor could come for diagnosis and treatment. Health education quickly became part of the mission. A state-of-the-art mobile disaster-relief unit, staffed by students, responds to the victims of earthquakes and other natural disasters.

Following the example of the medical school, other departments of the university began examining ways they might serve the people, especially the poor of the city. The law school established a program through which those unable to pay for legal services have their cases taken by students who must see their caseload through to completion before graduating. When presented with a legal problem, the student writes up the case and makes recommendations for the way it should be handled. This is reviewed by a committee of law professors, and private attorneys in the city also volunteer their time to advise the student advocates.

Education, business, and architecture followed suit. Dr. Garibay entitled these programs "Programas de Educación en la Comunidad" (Programs of Education in the Community) and wrote a two-volume book about their purpose, organization, history, obstacles, and successes, in 1979.

Today, Universidad Autónoma de Guadalajara is recognized the world over as one of the true pioneers in uniting academic study and volunteer community service and in demonstrating the good which comes to students, communities, their nation and the world when powerful and successful institutions make a strong commitment to the practice of service-learning.[10]

KODAIKANAL CHRISTIAN COLLEGE (KCC), TAMIL NADU, INDIA

The mission of Kodaikanal Christian College, founded in 1994, in the state of Tamil Nadu, India, is value education and service-learning. Though headed by an Indian Christian, Dr. Francis Soundararaj, Kodaikanal has a student body representative of the various religious traditions of India, particularly Hinduism and Islam. Himself a distinguished educator, Dr. Soundararaj had been principal of the old and prestigious Madras Christian College. When given the opportunity to direct a new college upon the principles not only of academic excellence but also service, he seized the chance. "Higher education," he declared, "will do well to promote the holistic development of young men and women without discarding the rigorous academic temper and approach in order to promote quality of life." To fulfill this precept, the college now requires that its students take service-learning courses that teach skills not normally acquired through a standard collegiate education. The courses and the service on which the college focuses deal with the education, health, and environmental issues affecting the tribal people of nearby Palani Hills.

India

---

10. Having learned of UAG's leadership in service-learning and in international education, The International Partnership for Service-Learning selected UAG as the site in Mexico for a program. The program has operated continuously—summer, fall, and spring semesters—since 1989.

The tribal people of the Palani Hills are made up of two different groups, the Paliars and the Puliars. These people live in remote jungle areas and depend on the forest for their daily food. About one hundred years ago most of these people were forced into bonded labor in the nearby coffee estates. It was to the benefit of the estate owners to keep the people uneducated and unsophisticated. Despite the outlawing of bonded labor, the practice continues, and the education of these people has been neglected and even actively opposed. The commitment of Kodaikanal to help these bonded laborers has been an act of courage for the institution and the individuals involved.

Schools are inaccessible to most of the people of the Palani Hills. Students have to make long journeys to attend even the closest schools. Families regard education as wasted time because the children are not making money, and many students drop out of school because the knowledge they already have is considered unimportant in traditional philosophy. Therefore, Kodaikanal's service-learning program focuses on educating these people.

To initiate its service-learning program, Kodaikanal adopted five villages: Kombakkadu, Venkatachalaparai, Vadakaraiparai, Vadakavunchi, and Bonded Labourers' Shed. Although each has a different socio-economic situation, all are extremely poor and lack educational facilities. As Kodaikanal officials approached the villages for discussion of how they might be of help, one villager decided to give up his hut so that a school might be developed in it. In response, the college created Kodaikanal Christian Tribal School, which now enrolls twenty-nine regular students and has been operating for over a year. In addition to the teaching, which is performed by KCC students, the college provides the schoolchildren with one free meal a day.

As a result of the Tribal School, the villagers' attitudes toward education are changing. They are beginning to see the importance of education and feel connected to the school. Conversely, the volunteers' perception of these tribal peoples has changed.

Students from wealthy families who never even knew about tribal lifestyles, or faced the realities of bonded labor, now have new, more realistic views.

Kodaikanal is doing more, however, than just teaching the children in the community. It is committed to building villagers' pride, history, and self-knowledge. The University is creating new textbooks that recount the legends of the tribes and describe cultural ceremonies important to these people. Nature classrooms are planned to draw upon tribal knowledge about the ecology of the jungle in which they live. Students are also working to help villagers obtain services from the government to which they are legally entitled, but of which the villagers have little awareness.

Kodaikanal's dedication to its surrounding community shows a college with both its students and the social needs of the region in mind. The students gain practical and philosophical knowledge about the nature of life in the rural hill country of Tamil Nadu, and the lives of the villagers in the Palani Hills have been improved by the commitment of the college, its leadership, faculty and students.

CRICHTON COLLEGE, THE UNIVERSITY OF GLASGOW, DUMFRIES, SCOTLAND

The University of Glasgow is one of Europe's oldest and most honored universities. Founded in 1451, the medieval buildings of the old campus, which still stand today on a hill overlooking the city, and the architecture of college buildings of each succeeding age, tell the story of its proud history. Glasgow is the alma mater of Joseph Lister, Adam Smith, Lord Kelvin, and countless other scientists and scholars of world renown.

Scotland

Now the University of Glasgow is pioneering institutional commitment to service-learning. It has opened a new three-year college, Crichton College, in Dumfries, which seeks to give students a broad-based education combining classroom learning with experiential education. For the past one hundred years, Glasgow has had a strong community-service program. It was not until 1991, however, that this program became integrated into the academic experience.[11]

The Department of Social Policy and Social Work, headed by Professor Rex Taylor, began a service-learning program in which students study British Social Policy and perform fifteen to twenty hours of service per week in a community agency. Students research the history of the agency at which they work, analyzing its governance, clients, operation, and effectiveness. The service is tied directly to issues discussed in the course, thereby giving the discussions relevance. The course enables students to have a deeper, richer understanding of both the agency and the social issues with which they are involved. The combination of service and study was recognized by Professor Taylor, who heads Crichton College, to be so powerful that the new college will make service-learning a centerpiece.

The mission of Crichton College states it will "prepare students with skills in reasoning, analysis and communication, with an appreciation of history and culture, a sensitivity to people and their environments and a commitment to improving their communities." To this end, all students take a core course entitled "Issues in Contemporary Society," which alerts them to the state of the modern world and the many problems that exist. During the second semester, students must take either "The Environment and Sustainability" or "Perspectives on Modern Scotland." The first is designed to inform students about the state of the environment, pollution within it, and methods to save and improve it. The latter course focuses on social and cultural issues in modern Scotland. The combination of one of these courses with "Issues in Contemporary Society" provides students with the necessary framework in which to perform a full-fledged

---

11. With the initiation of the program of the International Partnership.

service internship during subsequent years at Crichton.

All Crichton students are required to complete internships in one of four critical areas: health and social care, education, the arts, or environmental conservation. In these internships, students will connect what they have learned in their core studies to community problems. Most internships will be performed during the student's third year at Crichton.

The University of Glasgow's approach to service-learning is unique and noteworthy. It demonstrates the "faculty as the entry" point path to service-learning in which one department initiates the interest in service-learning, spreads it to other departments, and then integrates it into an entire college.

TRINITY COLLEGE OF QUEZON CITY, PHILIPPINES

Located in a borough of metro-Manila, Trinity College of Quezon City was founded in 1963 to provide educational opportunity for poor refugees from the mountain provinces of the northern Luzon region who were fleeing from the danger of insurgency. The college now has an enrollment of three thousand and includes a small graduate school along with its comprehensive undergraduate curriculum. Today, service-learning lies at the very heart of its institutional mission. The college takes seriously its motto, "Developing Persons for Others," and puts teeth into the rhetoric through various service-learning programs.

Philippines

Coordinated service-learning programs began at the college in 1977 when the College of Nursing, headed by Dr. Ester Santos, started a medical clinic open to members of nearby squatters' communities. This clinic provides now, as it did then, services including cost-free diagnoses of illness and seminars on basic health care, nutrition, and family planning. Staffed by College of Nursing students and faculty, the clinic enriches both patients and students. The program became nationally known and the College of Nursing at Trinity is recognized as having pioneered field service in nursing and related health fields, now a requirement for all such programs in the Philippines.

Since that time, Trinity College has developed a large array of service-learning programs in which students from a variety of disciplines participate. Currently the college has identified six local communities with which to work. These communities are some of the poorest in the Philippines and benefit greatly from interaction with the College.

Under the rubric CAUSE (Community Allied Urban Services and Education), the college operates six programs. STEP (Skills Training and Enablement Program) began in 1978 and provides training in dressmaking, tailoring, cosmetology, electronics, and food technology to local residents. REAPED (Review Assistance Program for the Empowerment of Drop-outs) works with local children to help them pass national examinations for placement into school. Students provide tutoring for the local children in a variety of subjects. BEST (Business Education for Self-Reliance and Trade) trains over thirty people every six months in typing, bookkeeping, inventory tracking, and other skills necessary to maintain a small business. Project LIFE (Living Initiatives For Enablement) works with local communities to provide job training and employment.

Another example of the College's commitment to others is found in Project DEEP. Disabled Enablement and Empowerment Program provides a network of support for students with disabilities. Trinity College is known for its support of students with disabilities and has been named the Philippines' First Disabled-Friendly School. Students from all disciplines are involved in the program. Very few schools in the Philippines accept students with disabilities, and this program shows Trinity's goal of opening its doors to all people. Disabled students are integrated into the mainstream of life at Trinity. Begun by former president Dr. Rafael Rodriguez, the program won for the College the coveted Mambini Award in the Philippines.

Other programs of the college include the mushroom growing and marketing project of the biology and business departments and a service project under the direction of the chaplain serving the people displaced by the eruption of Mt. Pinatubo.

In an effort to develop "Persons for Others," Trinity is connecting students from various majors with a variety of service-learning projects in the local community. Nursing students use their medical knowledge; business students, their economics; education majors, their teaching ability. The College also expresses its mission by making education accessible to all people, including the poor and those with disabilities.

It was for these reasons that The International Partnership for Service-Learning selected Trinity as the university in the Philippines most suited to host international service-learning students. Regular semester and year programs of the Partnership have been supplemented by special summer programs for international students. Now students from ten nations (Canada, China, England, India, Indonesia, Japan, Korea, Taiwan, Thailand, and the United States) participate regularly in the program.

Under the leadership of the new president, Dr. Orlando B. Molina, Trinity hosted a faculty seminar sponsored by the United Board for Christian Higher Education in Asia and The International Partnership for Service-Learning for faculty from eight Asian nations to help them develop local service-learning programs on their own campuses. With its proud and long history of service-learning, Trinity College of Quezon City is continuing to extend its experience in service-learning to other universities in the Philippines and abroad.

IN CONCLUSION

All of the institutions analyzed here offer higher education a renewed and reformed picture of itself. Each of these universities saw struggles and hardships occurring directly outside its gates. Rather than build the gates higher and stronger, each decided to remove the barriers between college and community. Leaders at these schools felt and feel that teaching must include interaction with local neighborhoods and community issues in order to overcome these problems.

Other examples of institutional commitment might have been cited. These six were selected not only for the variety they represent in geographic location, but for the differences in their histories and resources; in their curricula and national systems of education; in the kinds of service they are performing; and in the cultures of their nations and communities. Some, old and prestigious, have had to shake loose tradition and forgo the comfort in the status quo that so often comes with success. Others, young and struggling, are accepting the challenge of stretching precious resources to include service-learning in the college mission and budget.

The institutionalization of service-learning at these schools occurred in different ways. While four were mostly initiated by the president, two were a combination of student and faculty leadership.[12] University-wide service-learning programs must ultimately gain support at all levels in order to become truly institutionalized. The above institutions show the sophistication and depth to which universities may commit themselves if they catch the vision and are but bold enough.

Each of these institutions has stepped bravely forward, making the commitment in an act of will to connect their institutions to the needs of the community, the nation and the world. They are addressing problems and alleviating suffering. They are bringing up a new generation of leaders who will understand that the purpose of education is not only personal advancement but service for the common good.

---

12. The International Partnership is proud to have been involved in the development of service-learning at four of these institutions.

CHAPTER VI

PRESENT AND FUTURE STATES

THE PRESENT STATE

> I have observed as one preparing teachers of social/political education (civic education) that conventional teaching does not seem to be very effective....Students should experience social/political problems and procedures for solving them....get involved, participate in real matters, develop responsibility, and critically reflect upon their authentic experiences.[13]

Germany

> The global and domestic concerns for service-learning are inflaming adherents with a vision of reality—that multicultural experiences and community service can be a building block for intellectual growth and transformation in civic responsibilities. A subtle revolution is taking place in education.[14]

Philippines

These words summarize the opinions of educators and what we believe is now taking place in many parts of the world. From the formal survey and data gathered over many years, it is clear that the sheer scope of the practice of connecting education to service in communities has, in the decade of the 1990s, been impressive. In most of the countries surveyed, from the so-called First World to the Third World, versions of service-learning are taking place. Even in those countries where the efforts are as yet fledgling, the motivation toward education reform that makes education the servant of the society is apparent. Something previously unnoticed is taking place in higher education. The search for a way to teach values, including those related to caring for the world, its peoples, societies and environment, and the search for ways to make learning active and applicable—both are of the highest concern to educators.

---

13. Letter from F. Klaus Koopman, Universitat Bremen, Germany
14. Letter from Deana R. Aquino, Dean of the College of Education at Trinity College of Quezon City, Philippines.

While we repeat the caveat of the introduction—that this report is but an *initial* look and that there is much that we do not yet know—we have reached tentative conclusions about the state of service-learning around the world.

East Asia
Southeast Asia
United States
Mexico

First, it is in Asia, including both East and Southeast Asian countries, and North America, especially the United States and Mexico, that the most advanced developments in service-learning are occurring. In these two areas of the world there is a variety of models in use and many patterns for organizing and delivering programs connecting service and reflective study. And, as in most movements, there is or soon may be, a critical mass that increases the momentum and creates exponential growth.

India
Indonesia

National service schemes in India, Indonesia, Mexico, and the United States exerted a strong impetus for service and its logical extension—service-learning.

Latin America

Service-learning is growing in Latin America, as social needs are all too apparent and the need for universities to involve themselves in addressing these needs is equally apparent. In Argentina, for example, the organization CENOC (Centro Nacional de Organizaciones de la Comunidad—National Center of Community Organizations) has been working with Argentine universities to develop service-learning. In Ecuador, Universidad San Francisco de Quito and Universidad Espíritu Santo in Guayaquil have made service-learning requirement for graduation. Mexican universities, given impetus by the national service scheme and inspired by the example of the prestigious Universidad Autónoma de Guadalajara, have long had or are developing programs of education in the community.

Argentina

Ecuador

Mexico

Africa

In Africa, human and social problems are visible to all. The Association of African Universities officially endorsed the Wingspread Resolutions, a sign of the interest in service-learning and commitment to values implied. The South Africa Joint Education Trust is working with universities there to develop service-learning, a project supported by the Ford Foundation.

South Africa

In the Middle East and in Muslim countries and universities of Africa, the service practicum is common in many fields, and volunteer service to those in need is growing, but service-learning as applying to many disciplines is yet on the horizon.

Middle East
Africa

In Israel, service is a common experience. Israeli men must serve in the military; Israeli women must select either military or community service between secondary school and university. The service ethic carries over into university education, where all are encouraged to participate in some form of nation-building. At Ben Gurion University, the Community Action Unit involves half of the thirteen thousand students. Its activities include tutoring children and adults; "Perakh," a big brother/big sister program matching Ben Gurion students with underserved children in the area; "Open Apartments," providing university students with housing in disadvantaged neighborhoods in exchange for running various social programs such as clubs for children and teenagers; and teaching English classes. Community Action Unit also serves the Bedouin Arabs in a number of ways, including tutoring.

Israel

Volunteer service is a tradition in many European countries, especially the northern ones, as it is in Australia, and a good number of students take part. Swedish students are found around the world performing service as part of various directly-related curricula. Service is connected to some disciplines as in the traditional internships of social work.

Europe
Australia
Sweden

But in Europe, the example of Roehampton Institute London and Crichton, of the University of Glasgow, is unusual. The diploma program of the University of Montpellier, which is service-learning based, is a breakthrough in connecting academic study and community service.

England
Scotland
France
China
Russia
Kazakhstan
Kyrgyz Republic
Tajikistan

The present and former socialist countries—China, Russia, the Central Asian Republics, and former member states of the Soviet bloc—have a special challenge. Under the socialist model,

Turkmenistan
Uzbekistan
Hungary
Poland
Romania
Slovakia

with its strong emphasis on working for the good of the whole society rather than for the individual, service is usually required. It was (and in some countries still is) common practice for the government to announce that students from a particular university, residents of a neighborhood, or workers in a particular factory would be conscripted for a day or several days to perform a needed task. Sources familiar with these countries report contradictory feelings on the part of those taking part in required service.

On the one hand, for example, former participants recall their university's service days with some happy feelings—leaving the classroom and library to go to the country for harvest, camping in a barn, singing in the truck, dressing informally and generally enjoying the camaraderie of fellow students. They remember being proud of what was accomplished and that the needs of the people of the region were basically met. But conversely, there remains a deep-seated resentment—one might say anger—about having been forced by the government to take on hard tasks with no voice in the choice of activity or the timing of the service.

While, of course, opinions vary widely on the future, most seem to feel that there will be no turning back from the freedoms won in the past decade. The task for these nations now is to find ways of meeting the needs of the society and of individuals other than through conscripted service. The problems are enormous as people formerly cared for by the state are left without support. Newspapers in the central Asian republics, for example, report daily on suicides of elderly people who have no means of financial support.

Kyrgyz Republic In the Kyrgyz Republic, reputedly the most liberal and advanced of the five Central Asian Republics, a volunteer service movement shows signs of a tentative beginning. Women, for example, have formed support groups to help other women, and universities are developing their own chapters of these groups.

In the Czech Republic, the volunteer service movement is well underway. Homes and schools for the disabled and those with mental handicapping conditions are flooded with volunteers.

Czech Republic

But the use of volunteers, commendable as it is, is no solution to the problems facing these or other societies. It will take all of the powerful institutions of the society—government, business, religion, education, non-governmental organizations of all sorts—working together if the problems are to be managed and successfully addressed.

A second and clear observation from the survey and other data is that these developments are taking place spontaneously. To an informed observer, advocates and practitioners of service-learning in each nation are following a generalized concern with education and with the problems faced by their communities, nation and the world. They are essentially unaware of similar initiatives in other countries. The positive effect of this spontaneous and independent development is that service-learning is seen as a response to local concerns, and is no mere replication of an admired system of education.

The negative side of the independent generation of service-learning is that successful practices and powerful models are fragmented and not shared. The wheel is being reinvented over and over again. There is little or no cross-fertilization. Even within most nations, there have been few conferences, publications or meetings focused on connecting study and service. There are two notable exceptions. In the United States, organizations such as Campus Compact, The International Partnership for Service-Learning, the American Association for Higher Education, the National Society for Experiential Education and the Council of Independent Colleges have regularly published materials and held conferences on service-learning. A second country worth noting is India, where a national conference was held in 1998 on service-learning, organized by Mani Jacob, the

United States

India executive director of the All India Association for Christian Higher Education, an organization with 225 member colleges. The reverence of the nation for Gandhi, who called university students to service, and the National Service Scheme, in which one-fourth to one-third of Indian students participate, made Indian colleges receptive to the idea for the conference.

A third and encouraging conclusion is that service-learning in most places does not seem to be linked to a single political point of view. Institutions which are labeled "leftist" and those labeled "rightist" in their particular societies are alike adopting service-learning. Further, it should be noted that the distinctions between advocacy and service are blurred in most agencies. For example, the professionals and other staff working in agencies addressing the needs of poor children work to relieve the children's present suffering, redress their disadvantages, and at the same time act as their spokesmen to the government, schools, and other institutions of society which have power over the welfare of children. Colleges and universities which have instituted service-learning are, for the most part, not stepping directly into the role of advocate nor are they promoting a single approach to a problem. Rather, they are staying true to the academic mission of developing the skills of critical inquiry and allowing students to reach their own conclusions through the experience of study and service, and decide individually how to respond to the needs thus identified.

A fourth conclusion is that institutions thirst for opportunities for sharing and for the cross-fertilization that comes from the exchange of ideas and experiences. They want to know, and believe they would benefit from knowing, what is happening at other institutions and in other countries.

Institutions are frank in citing three reasons for sharing information. One is to learn from the experiences of others. They acknowledge that there are similar problems around the world, often of a global nature, and that institutions of higher education share a common organizational structure as well as common missions. Educators recognize that programs connecting colleges and universities with the issues of their communities in one part of the world may provide an adaptable model for use half a world away.

A second reason colleges and universities seek association with others engaged in service-learning is that many who are guiding these initiatives struggle for recognition of their efforts on their own campuses. The opportunity to describe and publicize their programs to an international audience would act to widen and deepen the support in their own institution.

A third reason, and perhaps the most important of all, is the need of educators to discuss with their colleagues ideas for the reform of education. Their interest in service-learning goes beyond that of a worthwhile program. It is part of a larger and more comprehensive motivation. College and university officials across nations are expressing their discontent and distress at the chasm between the academy and local, national and international communities. They believe that we must rethink the purposes of higher education in relation to the development of values, the building of leaders and citizens, and the training of active, inquiring minds of people who will then apply their skills to the needs of their own communities and of the world. They see service-learning as a strategy for attacking these all-important issues.

Just as they seek contacts for themselves in other nations, so they recognize the need for their students to experience the world beyond their own borders. Ipe M. Ipe, the principal of the highly selective St. John's College in Agra, India, has declared: "What our students lack is an opportunity to experience social conditions prevailing in other countries. For India, with a diverse cultural and religious background, this type of experience is essential for our students."

India

Other educators share the wish to involve their institution, students and faculty in intercultural and international service and studies. Their comments reflect a keen awareness that the growing international nature of the world demands that an understanding of that change is essential to being an educated person today.

The experience of service seems to be a powerful means of introducing students to global issues. The adage "think globally, act locally" was amended at the Wingspread Conference by David Peacock of Roehampton Institute London to "think globally, act wherever you are," an amendment accepted by all present.

NEXT STEPS

As the Wingspread Conference participants evaluated the potential of uniting academic study and volunteer service, and as they assessed its present state within higher education around the world, they also identified what might be needed to give greater momentum to this incipient but potentially powerful movement in higher education. They determined that, above all, the separate colleges and universities need to be brought together through an international organization to give visibility and prestige to the efforts being made on individual campuses.

They articulated the need to give recognition to the outstanding contributions of students and of community agencies through service-learning. They speculated on ways new technology could be utilized in service. They developed a plan for publications and for international conferences, and they drew up an organizational structure to make these activities happen. In short, they asked—and answered—the question of what steps need to be taken to bring the common goals of these disparate efforts into a coherent network.

The Wingspread Plan, refined by the task force appointed by

the conference participants, first asked the board of trustees if they would allow the transformation of the International Partnership for Service-Learning so that it might serve as the coordinating framework.

A first plank of the Plan called for the inclusion of more institutions around the world, and that the work of advancing service-learning be carried out through local chapters on individual college and university campuses. It asked that the new International Partnership develop a certificate program through which Partnership chapters could reward their outstanding service-learning students and recognize cooperation of their partner service agencies.

A second item was that of advocacy through publications and conferences. The recommendation was for a regularly published journal and newsletter to be widely disseminated which would highlight the theory and practice of service-learning, and that the editorial board of the journal and authorship of articles be truly international.

The suggestion was made that international conferences be held every two years (succeeding the previously held annual conferences) and that each conference would target and be held in another part of the world. It was requested that smaller faculty seminars be sponsored to train teachers in the means of joining study with service and that the team of trainers be international.

The plan asked that the use of distance-learning, electronic mail, and other new technologies be investigated to see if and how these devices might serve the cause of service-learning.

The plan called for more "flagship" programs sponsored by the International Partnership with students of many nations participating together. It was urged that funding be sought to enable the participation of students from developing countries. First World institutions were encouraged to help support other institutions and also to find the funds from their own institutional budgets to allow their students to participate—a sign of institutional commitment.

It was recognized that all the suggested programs and activities might be best accomplished through cooperation with other organizations. We were reminded to take a lesson from international business—that the critical mass necessary for effectiveness is created by collaboration.

Finally, there was the request that the governing board be made international and include representatives of service agencies.

PARTNERSHIP ACTIONS

Since the Wingspread Conference in May, 1998, many of these recommended steps have been initiated. The Board of Trustees accepted unanimously the challenge of transformation, and began by electing trustees from Ecuador, England, Egypt, and Mexico, including a representative of an important NGO, Children International.

Local chapters, given the title "Distinguished Partner," are being formed in universities around the world. The campus chapters are made up of high level administrators, faculty, service or service-learning coordinators, study abroad directors, and student leaders. They are setting about the task of developing service-learning on their own campuses with the goal of institutionalization.

A first and pleasurable task for the chapters is to recommend, for review by an international committee of the Partnership, two students from their campus to receive the international certificate for distinguished service and learning, to choose the community agency that they wish to honor, and to arrange for the public presentation of the awards which will be given annually.

An international editorial committee for the journal has been formed, headed by Indian scholar, poet, and translator Kalyan Ray, with the first volume to be published in the spring of 2000. The newsletter *Action/Reflection* is sent internationally.

The Wingspread plan for biennial conferences will focus on Latin America in the year 2000 and be held in Ecuador; on Europe, including Eastern Europe, in 2002 and be held in Prague; and on Asia in 2004. A week-long seminar in the Philippines for faculty from eight nations and eighteen institutions was held in cooperation with the United Board for Christian Higher Education in Asia with follow-up through an Internet list-serve.

The new technologies pose a challenge and an opportunity for the advocates of service-learning. The use of distance learning has long been criticized for its individualistic method and failure to provide for the socialization of students. Combining academic study and the international exchange of ideas via the Internet with local service will provide students and faculty with both intellectual stimulus and the interaction with others that leads to personal growth. The Partnership is working in cooperation with an international organization to develop service-learning studies and shared experiences to be offered via the World Wide Web.

The Partnership is exploring new program sites and is working with other organizations to offer programs to students of many nations. Programs in the summer of 1998 and 1999 brought students from fourteen nations, mostly developing countries, to learn and serve together in three locations—Canada, England, and the Philippines.

Finally, the Partnership seeks organizations that will join in making known the promise service-learning holds for the reform of education, for meeting social and human needs and for building caring, committed, and capable leadership for the future. The Centre for Global Leadership, successor to the United Nations Leadership Academy, headed by Adel Safty and headquartered in Egypt, and AFS-USA, headed by Alex Plinio, are two such organizations developing joint programs with the International Partnership.

Egypt
United States

YOUR CHALLENGE

Educators at all levels, but perhaps especially those in higher education, must commit their resources, including facilities, finances, faculty expertise, and the energy, idealism, and intelligence of their students, to the tasks of the society.

For those educators and institutions so willing (as are those courageous leaders described in Chapter V and many of those cited previously), the result is a revitalized institution and a renewed energy for teaching and learning. When service to the society is brought to the very heart of the teaching and learning enterprise, there is for faculty and students alike the belief that what they learn and what they do with what they learn matters. The service makes the learning immediate, relevant, and of critical importance; the study and reflection informs the service.

From our own experiences and observations, and those of colleagues around the world, we have identified three major dimensions of service-learning which justify its consideration as a strategy deserving a central position in educational change.

First, as a pedagogy, service-learning speaks to the core of needed educational reform, responding to the new developments in cognitive science as to how the mind works and how learning actually takes place. It brings teaching and learning, faculty and students, disciplines and content, into new relationships and understanding. The student relationship with faculty becomes collaborative rather than hierarchical. The disciplines are seen as lenses through which to interpret the world rather than as ends in themselves. Faculty learn the skills and benefits of

Present and Future States   93

collaboration for common educational goals. Learning becomes active rather than passive. "Students are allowed to be present at their own education."[15]

Additionally, service-learning students forsake the stance of the uninvolved "objective" observer, merely putting in time until receiving the needed credentials. They discover their own talents, the rewards of service to those in need, the purpose for their own lives, and, through their personal involvement, learn they are needed and have a job to do. While they realize, correctly, that they cannot single-handedly change the world, they also realize that each person may and must contribute to the good of the whole. And they accept that education is not merely for personal gain and public renown. They discover education's nobler purpose, and that the privilege of higher education carries with it a responsibility to apply one's learning to the good of those not so privileged. In the words of Christopher Walsh, former deputy principal of Whitelands College, in England, "Through service-learning knowledge is transformed into wisdom."

England

In the end, the impact of service-learning is deeper even than connections made between studies and service, college and community, theory and practice, learning and doing. Service-learning has to do with attitudes and behaviors that lie at the root of how a society functions. Wrote one president of a university of the Carpathian region of Eastern Europe,[16] "The first impact of this initiative of service-learning is spiritual; it is about motivation, about feeling responsibility towards the local and larger community. It reinforces speaking not only in financial or academic terms, but in terms of service."

Carpathia

---

15. Knefelkamp, Lee, Keynote Address, IPS-L Conference. March 1, 1991, St. Louis, Missouri, U.S.
16. From *Carpathia Project Report: Building Bridges Between Institutions of Higher Education in the Carpathian Region of East Central Europe and the Southeastern United States: First Phase Report*. From the Associated Colleges of the South, sponsored with USAID.

Two related values that service-learning cultivates are those of collaboration and trust. These values are not mere sentimentality, but lie at the foundation of social structures and development. Francis Soundararaj, principal of Kodaikanal College in India, has written:[17]

India

> Human and material resources often become meagre owing to the failure to share them. The same reasons which have widened the gap between the rich and the poor hold good to explain the paucity of resources in individual institutions and sectors. Duplication of services and programmes, closeness of institutions not to share resources, and the concentration of resources in particular institutions have created an artificial scarcity...Consortium ties, networking, twinning, adoption of villages by universities, consultancies, the creation of community colleges, philanthropy and pledging—all are means to promote sharing. Service-learning is an example, modeling a behaviour and approach which focus on sharing.

Africa

And Richard Sack, the Executive Director of the Association for the Development of Education in Africa has written:[18]

> Trust, we are coming to understand, is an essential building block for development. This is being increasingly explored by scholars of development, some of whom refer to it as the base of the "social capital" required for development....Intuitively, we know that education is based on partnerships and trust...between teacher and learner, school and community....Partnerships and trust imply maximum sharing of information; transparency and the full involvement of all participating,...enabl[ing] them to feel that they have a stake in both the process and its outcomes; and identifying clearly one's partners.

Service-learning teaches these values. At its core, service-learning is a collaboration between agencies and the communi-

---

17. Francis Soundararaj, "The Sharing of Resources," a paper delivered at the Consultation on Higher Education: CSI Golden Jubilee, December, 1997 in Mavelikara, Kerala, India.
18. Richard Sack, 1999. Communicating about Education: Partnerships, Trust and Pedagogy. ADEA Newsletter (Association for the Development of Education in Africa), V. 11, N. 2.

ties they serve; between university and agency, between student and teacher, and among them all. Students see the results when the institutions of a society work together to address problems. They are witness to the intentions and to the negotiating that must occur for the needs of all to be met.

As students observe the agency and university in action and are themselves a part of the collaboration, they see the work and commitment which goes into the building of trust, and that such trust is often hard-won. The success of an agency's effort is dependent on the trust it is able to generate in the people it means to serve. Students find out that their acceptance comes as they prove their own trustworthiness. These lessons are essential to the building of mature and responsible lives and are equally necessary in the building of the social fabric.

What greater mission can higher learning serve than the teaching of these values and skills?

What better method can be found than the joining of academic study and volunteer community service?

We invite you, the reader, to join this international movement, for the re-forming of the profession of education that you love and to which you are committed, and for a better world, which together we may build in the new millennium.

APPENDIX I

ACKNOWLEDGMENTS

The International Partnership for Service-Learning is grateful to:

The Ford Foundation, and especially to Alison Bernstein, Vice President for Education, Media, Arts and Culture, for a long commitment to service-learning in the United States and abroad, for support of the International Partnership over the years, and most recently for support of the Wingspread Conference and the consequent production and dissemination of this study of service-learning around the world.

The Johnson Foundation at Wingspread for support of many projects related to the development of service-learning and especially of the 1998 Wingspread Conference "Constructing the World Anew."

The staff of the International Partnership, especially Alex Tinari, Coordinator of Special Projects, who helped organize the Wingspread Conference and mailed and processed the surveys; her able successor, Erika Ryser, who translated from Spanish, edited *An Initial Look* and organized the distribution; David Janes, Director of College and University Relations, who wrote the material for Chapter IV; and Christoph Berenbroick, Coordinator of Student Programs, for supplying student information.

Those helping with the production, Preston Merchant, designer of the Wingspread publications and of the cover of *An Initial Look*; and Kate Egan Norris for her work as copy editor of this study.

The trustees of the International Partnership and the program directors, faculty and service agency supervisors affiliated with the Partnership, who have over many years supplied information about service-learning, *and*

The following persons, who filled in questionnaires and otherwise furnished material about service-learning in their institutions, regions, and nations, and through their organizations.

ARGENTINA
Centro Nacional de Organizaciones de la Comunidad, Buenos Aires
    Elizabeth Iñíguez

AUSTRALIA
New College, The University of New South Wales, Sydney
    Allan K. Beavis
Richard Johnson College, Wollongong
    Jeanette Donnan
Ridley College, University of Melbourne
    Stewart Gill
St. Martin's College, Charles Sturt University, Wagga Wagga
    Andrew Callander
University of Western Sydney
    Margaret Vickers

CANADA
Renison College, University of Waterloo, Ontario
    Gail Cuthbert Brandt

CHINA
Chung Chi College, The Chinese University of Hong Kong
    Rance P. L. Lee, Ngai Sek Yum
Hong Kong Baptist University
    Daniel C. W. Tse

CZECH REPUBLIC
Charles University, Prague
    Marie Cerna

DENMARK
Aalborg University, Aalborg
    Sven Casperson

ECUADOR
Universidad Espíritu Santo, Guayaquil
    Albert Eyde, Irma Guzmán, Johnnie González

Universidad Laica Vicente Rocafuerte, Guayaquil
    Elsa Alarcón Soto
Universidad San Francisco de Quito
    María del Carmen Molestina, Diego Quiroga

EGYPT
Centre for Global Leadership, Cairo
    Adel Safty

ENGLAND
Bishop Grosseteste College Lincoln
    Eileen Baker, Jim Tarpey
Canterbury Christ Church College, University of Kent
    Michael Wright, Brian Kelly
Imperial College, University of London
    Sinclair Goodlad
King Alfred's Winchester
    John P. Dickinson
University College Chester
    Tim Wheeler, Lesley E. Cooke
University College of Ripon and York St. John, Univ. of Leeds, York
    Robin Butlin, K. Reedy
Roehampton Institute London, University of Surrey
    David Peacock, Peter Wesson, Jenny Iles

FRANCE
University of Montpellier
    Chantal Thery

GERMANY
Universistat Bremen, Bremen
    Klaus Koopmann

HUNGARY
Debrecen Agricultural University
    Zsolt Nemessalyi
Godollo Univerisity of Agriculture
    Gyorgy Heltai, Beata P. Sandor

University of Miskole
    Miklos Szabo
Lajos Kossuth University, Debrecen
    Sandor Nagy

INDIA
American College, Madurai
    Peter Jayapandian, P. Pandiyaraja
    R. Dinakaran Michael, V. Swaminathan
Bishop Heber College, Tiruchirapalli
    G. Edwin Chandrasekaran
C.S.I. Ewart Women's Christian College, Chennai
    Premila Chandrasekaran
Isabella Thoburn College, Lucknow
    E. S. Charles
Kattakada Christian College, Kerala
    D. Christudas, Lucy Paul
Kittel Science College, Dharwad
    John S. Kuri
Kodaikanal Christian College, Kodaikanal
    Francis Soundararaj, J. Sam Daniel Stalin
Lady Doak College, Madurai
    Nirmala Jeyaraj, Mercy Pushpalatha
Madras Christian College
    M. Gladstone, Vasanthi Vijayakuman
Sarah Tucker College, Tirunelveli
    Mercy Henry
St. Christopher's College of Education, University of Madras
    Vimala Earnest Punithakumar
St. John's College, Agra
    Ipe M. Ipe
St. John's College, Palayamkottai
    J. Balasingh
St. Xavier's College, Tamil Nadu
    Anthony A. Pappuraj
Stella Maris College, Chennai
    Pauline Swaminathan

Women's Christian College, Madras
   Kanmani Christian

INDONESIA
Pelita Harapan University, Jakarta
   Willi Toisuta
Petra Christian University, Surabaya
   Aris Pongtuluran, Rahardjo Tirtoatmodjo, Pietra Widiadi
Satya Wacana University, Salatiga
   Krishna Djaya Darumurti

ISRAEL
Ben Gurion University of the Negev, Beer-Sheva
   Mark Gelber, Rebecca Weinstein

JAMAICA
University of Technology, Kingston
   Rae A.Davis, Omar Brown
   Veta Lewis, Carmen Pencle

JAPAN
Heian Jogakuin College, Osaka
   Paul Makoto Goto, Seiji Yoshioka
International Christian University, Tokyo
   Koa Tasaka
Kobe International University
   Isai Sasaki, O'Donnell
Nagoya Ryujo Junior College
   Takeo
Rikkyo University, Tokyo
   David Osamu Tsukada, Herbert Donovan
Sophia University, Tokyo
   Keiji Otami, Yoshihiko Miwa
St. Luke's College of Nursing, Tokyo
   Shigeaki Hinohara
Tokyo Woman's Christian University
   Masako Sanada

JORDAN
United Nations University Leadership Academy, University of Jordan, Amman
    Adel Safty

KOREA
Ewha Woman's University, Seoul
    Sang Chang, Soung Yee Kim, Hyun-Hye Lee
Hannam University, Taejon
    Won-Bae Kim
Seoul Women's University
    Gui-woo Lee
Soongsil University, Seoul
    Yoon-Bae Ouh, Moon-Kyum Kim
    Tai Young Park
Sungkonghoe University, Seoul
    Jae Joung Lee

KYRGYZ REPUBLIC
American University, Bishkek
    Martha Merrill
International University, Bishkek
    Martha Merrill

LIBERIA
Cuttington University College, Suacoco
    Melvin J. Mason

MEXICO
Universidad Autónoma de Guadalajara
    Alvaro Romo de la Rosa, José Luis Arreguín
    Guadalupe Delgadillo

PHILIPPINES
Central Philippine University, Iloilo City
    Juanito M. Acanto, Nathaniel M. Fabula
    Melvin M. Mangana

Easter College, Baguio City
    Marilyn L. Ngales, Frances K. Laoyan
Silliman University, Damaguete City
    Agustin A. Pulido, Maria Teresita Sy-Simda
    Jesusa Corazon L.P. Gonzalez, Enrique Oracion
Trinity College of Quezon City
    Orlando Molina, Erlinda G. Rosales

POLAND
Pedagogical University Rzeszow
    Kazimierz Sowa
Technical University of Rzeszow
    Szczepan Wolinski, Marian Granops
Technical University of Lublin
    Iwo Pollo
University of Mining and Metallurgy, Krakow
    Andrzej Golas

ROMANIA
Babes-Bolyai University, Cluj-Napoca
    Paul Servan Agachi

SCOTLAND
Crichton University, Dumfries
    Rex Taylor
University of Glasgow
    Stewart Asquith, Susan Deeley

SLOVAKIA
University of P.J. Safarik
    Lev Bukovsky
Kosice Technical University
    Karol Florian, Tomas Sabol
Kosice University of Veterinary Medicine
    Marta Prosbova
Letna 9, Kosice
    Anton Lavrin

SOUTH AFRICA
University of Witwatersrand, Johannesburg
    Colin Bundy
Joint Education Trust, Johannesburg
    Nicholas Taylor

TAIWAN
Soochow University, Taipei
    Hann-Jong Chueh
St. John's and St. Mary's Institute of Technology, Tamsui
    Andrew C. Chang, Yu-li Lee
Tunghai University, Taichung
    Lin Li-Sheng

THAILAND
Payap University, Chiang Mai
    Boonthong Poocharoen, Martha Butt
    Yuthachai Damrongmanee

UGANDA
Makerere University, Kampala
    Eliphaz Maari
Uganda Christian University, Mukono
    Eliphaz Maari, Alex Kagume-Mugisha

UKRAINE
State University Lviv Polytechnic
    Yuriy Rudavsky, Jurij Rashkevich

UNITED STATES
Campus Compact, Providence, Rhode Island
    Elizabeth Hollander
Hobart and William Smith Colleges, Geneva, New York
    Richard Hersh, Jay Mapstone
Jamestown Community College, Jamestown, New York
    Margaret Gwynne
Macalester College, St. Paul, Minnesota
    Michael McPherson

South Dakota State University (Lakota Nation), Brookings
    Valerian Three Irons
St. Augustine College, Chicago, Illinois
    Carlos A. Plazos
St. Augustine's College, Raleigh, North Carolina
    Bernard W. Franklin, Olivia E. Jones
St. Paul's College, Lawrenceville, Virginia
    Thomas M. Law, Laughton D. Thomas
Trinity College, Hartford, Connecticut
    Evan Dobelle
United States Naval Academy, Annapolis, Maryland
    Eleanor G. Chisholm
University of the South, Sewanee, Tennessee
    Samuel R. Williamson, S. Dixon Myers
Voorhees College, Denmark, South Carolina
    Leonard E. Dawson, Tanesha Jackson

And to the following who contributed information from international organizations and special international projects:

Associated Colleges of the South, United States/Carpathian Universities
    Dixon Myers, Wayne Anderson
Association of African Universities
    Melvin Mason
Central Asian Republics of the Kyrgyz Republic, Kazakhstan, Tajikistan, Turkmenistan and Uzbekistan
    Martha Merrill
Colleges and Universities of the Anglican Communion
    John C. Powers
International Association of University Presidents
    Sven Capersen, Alvaro Romo de la Rosa
National Service Scheme of India
    Mani Jacob
Peer Tutoring International
    Pia MacRae
United Board for Christian Higher Education in Asia
    David Vikner

APPENDIX II

ABOUT THE INTERNATIONAL PARTNERSHIP FOR SERVICE-LEARNING

The International Partnership for Service-Learning, founded in 1982, is an incorporated not-for-profit education organization, with headquarters in New York, whose mission is to foster and develop programs linking community service and academic study in institutions of higher education around the world.

The International Partnership holds that joining study and service:
- is a powerful means of learning
- addresses human needs that would otherwise remain unmet
- promotes intercultural and international knowledge and understanding
- gives expression to the obligation of public and community service by educated people
- sets academic institutions in right relationship to the larger society.

The International Partnership initiates, designs and administers off-campus programs combining service and academic study, open to qualified undergraduate students and recent graduates of all nations. Current programs of a semester, year or summer are offered in affiliation with partner universities in the Czech Republic, Ecuador, England, France, India, Israel, Jamaica, Mexico, the Philippines, Scotland and South Dakota, U.S. (with Native Americans). Programs in other locations are being developed. The Partnership also sponsors a Master's Degree in International Service to prepare professionals for work in international non-governmental relief and development organizations.

The International Partnership advises on the development of local service-learning programs, making known the opportunities and experience of service-learning through research, publications, international and regional conferences, and faculty seminars. The newsletter, *Action/Reflection*, promotes service-learning and describes current activities.

Governed by an international board of trustees made up of university presidents, service agency professionals and leaders in higher education, the International Partnership is staffed by full-time professionals who oversee the programs, organize the publications, and plan the conferences and other related activities.

The International Partnership for Service-Learning has been supported with grants from the Ford Foundation, the Henry Luce Foundation, the Hitachi Foundation and NAFSA: Association of International Educators.

The International Partnership for Service-Learning
815 Second Avenue, Suite 315
New York, NY 10017-4594 U.S.A.
Telephone 212-986-0989 Facsimile: 212-986-5039
pslny@aol.com

APPENDIX III

WINGSPREAD RESOLUTIONS AND LIST OF SIGNATORIES

Actions taken by the participants of an international conference
International Service-Learning: Constructing the World Anew
May 11-13, 1998

Wingspread
Racine, Wisconsin, USA

I. INTRODUCTION

For some years now and especially in the last decade, universities and colleges of higher education around the world have been developing programs for their students that link formal learning and volunteer community service.

Although diverse in history, location, curricula, student bodies and resources, these institutions are using the pedagogy of service-learning to re-connect their institutions to the needs of their community by working cooperatively with community organizations. They have discovered that service-learning has the power to reform education, transform students, and address human and social needs.

In May 1998, forty-one leaders in higher education and social service organizations from fifteen nations met at Wingspread (Wisconsin, USA) to design an international organization whose mission would be to promote and support the development of service-learning.

Supported by the Ford Foundation and the Johnson Foundation, the conference was convened by The International Partnership for Service-Learning. A non-governmental, not-for-profit educational organization founded in 1982 and with headquarters in New York, The International Partnership offers service-learning programs in eleven nations for students (of any nation) at the bachelor's and master's degree levels, and advocates the joining of service and learning through conferences, publications and faculty training opportunities.

During the deliberations, the Wingspread Conference participants reviewed draft resolutions formulated by a committee headed by David Peacock. Revisions were made and at the conclusion of the conference participants unanimously approved their adoption.

The approved resolutions, with a list of the signatories, follows:

II. THE RESOLUTIONS

Preamble: Over recent years, as a result of work carried out in a significant and growing number of countries across the world, the power and value of students in higher education learning through service has become evident. Moreover, it has become evident that institutions in different parts of the world have developed a range of creative and innovative strategies for the development of programmes of service-learning. These programmes might usefully and profitably be shared at the international level both by those institutions already committed to the provision of these programmes and by those institutions interested in the introduction of service-learning programmes into their educational mission. It is with a view to enabling and encouraging the further development of service-learning within a context of global cooperation and interchange that the following proposals have been formulated.

Because:
- the major challenges facing human societies at the dawn of the third millennium are largely shared, and
- institutions of higher education, from their positions of relative privilege and influence, ought properly to be committed to the relief of human suffering and the enhancement of quality of life for all, and
- the idealism and energy, especially among the young, motivate people to seek social change and the creation of a better world, and
- the value of experiential learning at higher education level is now widely recognised, and

- societies across the world depend to a greater or lesser extent on the voluntary principle to provide care and support for their members

Therefore:
We, as representatives of universities and colleges of higher education and of social service organisations from across the world with an existing commitment to the continued development of learning through service, seek continuing association in a spirit of mutual respect, co-operation, affirmation and support,

In order to:
- enable students from across the world to benefit from the advantages of programmes of service-learning, and
- encourage, in cooperation with communities, the continued development of service-learning in institutions of higher education and in service agencies across the world, and
- enable an international sharing of experience and good practice in the field, and
- achieve a wider dissemination of the values and ideals of learning through service, and
- encourage institutions of higher learning to play their rightful role in both addressing local and global challenges and seeking to meet human and social needs, and
- promote a sense of community and civic responsibility, and
- advance the common purpose of building a new generation of leaders through service-learning, and
- encourage public policies which initiate and support opportunities for community service linked to the education of students

Will further these purposes through:
- the development of a broad network of contacts between and among academic institutions and social service organisations, and
- the establishment of appropriate and timely communication strategies, and
- the organisation of conferences and training opportunities, and
- curricular development aimed at enabling both staff and students in institutions to serve and learn in multicultural environments and to

gain cross-cultural experiences, and
- the fostering of local programmes of service-learning, and
- the fostering of joint programmes of international service-learning, and
- the encouragement of service-learning research projects

Do hereby:
Propose the development of an international network for service-learning, and

Thereto:
invite to join in the network all universities and colleges of higher education, social service organisations, and individuals wishing to work together with others as active partners in the furtherance of the network's goals.

Membership:
Open to all institutions, organisations, and individuals who have made a commitment to the principle and practice of service-learning.

Implementation:
In order to continue the work of the Wingspread conference, the conference participants do hereby appoint a Task Force and charge them with developing a plan for implementation, including a business plan, using where possible the ideas expressed at the Wingspread meeting, and to include
- developing a statement of the nature and intent of service-learning,
- establishing means of communication,
- designing structures of organisation and membership,
- surveying in so far as possible the extent and various models of service-learning as employed in institutions around the world,
- initiating activities which will further the goals,
- reporting regularly to the participants on progress, and
- seeking means of funding the activities.

Building on the experience, network, history and leadership of The International Partnership for Service-Learning, the conference participants request IPS-L professional staff to serve as secretariat and headquarters of the Task Force.

The conference participants further request the trustees of the Partnership to give their support by considering ways in which The International Partnership for Service-Learning may continue its commitment demonstrated through the organisation of the Wingspread conference to the international effort to develop service-learning.

III. THE SIGNATORIES

The Wingspread conference participants and signatories to the resolutions represent a wide variety of institutions of higher education and service organizations. From sixteen nations in Africa, Asia, Europe, the Middle East and the Americas, they represent organizations and institutions large and small, public and private, affluent and struggling, world-renowned and as yet locally known, secular and church-related. The signatories' primary affiliations are listed below, but all have multiple roles as they have been and are active leaders in related organizations.

Though diverse in culture, background, and types of institutions and organizations they represent, the signatories were of one mind in believing that academic institutions need to forge closer relations with communities, that educating students to be competent leaders who will work actively for the good of their societies is a primary task of higher education, and that an international partnership would be valuable in furthering the practice of service-learning around the world.

CZECH REPUBLIC
Marie Cerna, Head of the Special Education Department, Charles University

DENMARK
Sven Caspersen, Rector, Aalborg University

ECUADOR
Victor V. Maridueña, Executive Director, Children International - Ecuador
María del Carmen Molestina, Director of International Programs, Universidad San Francisco de Quito
Diego Quiroga, Dean of Academic Affairs, Universidad San Francisco de Quito

ENGLAND
Kevin Bales, Principal Lecturer, Roehampton Institute London
Pia MacRae, Manager, BP International Tutoring and Mentoring Project
David Peacock, Pro-Rector, Roehampton Institute London
Peter Wesson, Dean, Roehampton Institute London

FRANCE
Chantal Thery, Director of International Relations, Université Montpellier II

HONG KONG
Rance P.L. Lee, Head, Chung Chi College

INDIA
Mithra G. Augustine, Secretary, Association of Christian Institutes for Social Concern in Asia
Nirmala Jeyaraj, Principal, Lady Doak College

INDONESIA
Willi Toisuta, Advisor to the President, Pelita Harapan University

JAMAICA
Rae A. Davis, President, University of Technology
Veta C. Lewis, Head of the Technical Education Department, University of Technology
Carmen V. Pencle, Senior Lecturer, University of Technology

JORDAN
Adel Safty, Director of the International Leadership Academy, United Nations University

LIBERIA
Melvin J. Mason, Official Representative, Association of African University Presidents; President, Cuttington University College

MEXICO
José Luis Arreguín, Director of the International Office, Universidad Autónoma de Guadalajara
María Guadalupe Delgadillo, Head of the University Exchange Department, Universidad Autónoma de Guadalajara

PHILIPPINES
Erlinda G. Rosales, Vice-President for Academic Affairs, Trinity College of Quezon City

SOUTH AFRICA
Colin Bundy, Vice-Chancellor, University of the Witwatersrand
Nicholas C. Taylor, Executive Director, Joint Education Trust

SCOTLAND
Rex Taylor, Director, Crichton College of the University of Glasgow

UNITED STATES
Louis S. Albert, Vice-President, American Association for Higher Education
Howard A. Berry, President, The International Partnership for Service-Learning
Linda A. Chisholm, Vice-President, The International Partnership for Service-Learning
Martha E. Church, former Senior Scholar, The Carnegie Foundation for the Advancement of Teaching; former President, Hood College
Margaret A. Gwynne, Dean of Academic Affairs, Jamestown Community College
Elizabeth Hollander, Executive Director, Campus Compact

Patricia Hough, Cooperative Education Coordinator, Borough of Manhattan Community College
Florence E. McCarthy, Coordinator of the International Education Development Program, Columbia University Teachers College
Thomas E. Nyquist, President, Nyquist Associates; Mayor, Village of New Paltz, New York
Susan J. Poulsen, The Johnson Foundation at Wingspread
Margaret D. Pusch, Associate Director, Intercultural Communication Institute
Susan Stroud, Counselor to the CEO, The Corporation for National Service
Kalyan B. Ray, Associate Professor, County College of Morris
Alvaro Romo de la Rosa, Coordinator of International Programs, University of Houston System
Valerian Three Irons, Director of Service-Learning, South Dakota State University
Humphrey Tonkin, President, University of Hartford
David Vikner, President, United Board for Christian Higher Education in Asia

APPENDIX IV

DISTINGUISHED PARTNER PROGRAM

In May, 1999, at the annual meeting, the international board of trustees approved a plan to invite selected colleges and universities around the world to form local chapters of the International Partnership, to be named Distinguished Partners, and to award annually the International Certificate for Distinguished Service-Learning to its students and community agencies. The approved plan was first suggested at a 1998 meeting, held at the Wingspread Conference Center in the United States, of educators and service providers from 16 countries in Africa, the Americas, Asia, Europe and the Middle East who gathered to consider how service-learning might be expanded and deepened in institutions of higher education. The plan was refined by a task force appointed at Wingspread and then officially endorsed by the officers and trustees.

The Distinguished Partner Program is designed to further the initiation and development of service-learning and international education in institutions of higher education around the world. Distinguished Partner colleges and universities will be in the company of the world's most highly respected institutions of higher education. Each college and university which is designated a Distinguished Partner forms a local chapter of the International Partnership which works to encourage local programs of service-learning, engagement in International Partnership for Service-Learning programs, conferences, and faculty development seminars, and awards International Certificates for Distinguished Service and Learning to students and community agencies.

The Distinguished Partner Program is not a membership program and therefore has no dues. Instead, the program is The International Partnership for Service-Learning's means of encouraging the development of service-learning world-wide. Partners promote local service-learning and the International Partnership provides support for and recognition of these programs. Colleges and Universities become Distinguished Partners by invitation of the International Partnership's international board of trustees.

Distinguished Partners form local chapters of The International Partnership for Service-Learning. These Chapters:
- Develop and implement plans to further service-learning locally
- Promote international/intercultural education
- Select two students and one community agency to receive certificates annually
- Arrange for the public awarding of certificates
- Involve the appropriate organizations and officials on campus and in the local community in the activities of the chapter
- Name the chapter, perhaps honoring someone connected to the institution or community who is a recognized public servant
- Report annually on the activities of the chapter
- Encourage where possible participation in Partnership programs and activities

Colleges and Universities named as Distinguished Partners are entitled to award annually the International Certificate for Distinguished Service and Learning to two students and one community agency. This certificates bears the names of the Charter Distinguished Partners and is internationally recognized. Each Chapter of the International Partnership is responsible for choosing recipients of the certificates and for publicly awarding them. Names of awardees are submitted to the headquarters of the International Partnership for Service-Learning two months prior to the public ceremony.

The International Partnership for Service-Learning administers a variety of programs of grants and scholarships. Distinguished Partners receive information about these special opportunities and, if eligible, are invited to participate.

The International Partnership for Service-Learning connects people and institutions interested in service-learning through a variety of publications, conferences, and training seminars. Distinguished Partners are part of this network and receive all publications without charge. Additionally, Distinguished Partners are especially highlighted in these publications and are invited to participate in conferences and seminars at a reduced fee.

In cooperation with the International Education and Resource Network (I*EARN) and with our Distinguished Partners, the International Partnership for Service-Learning is developing opportunities for learning using the World Wide Web. This program will enable students from many countries who are performing service locally to connect and study under the direction of an international faculty. The home faculty supervises the local service and determine how the learning will be credited or otherwise recognized.

DISTINGUISHED PARTNER PROGRAM

Colleges and universities may express interest in becoming Distinguished Partners, and submit an application. Once invited to become a Distinguished Partner, a college or university forms a local chapter of the International Partnership for Service-Learning by developing a committee. This committee consists of appropriate university officials, students, and community members who are invested in service-learning. Members might include a service-learning/community service director, international program directors, campus ministers, students, faculty, and/or local service agency directors. This group then draws up a plan to be submitted to the International Partnership, answering the following questions:

1. DISTINGUISHED PARTNER Describe the reasons your institution wants to be a Distinguished Partner and how this program will assist your college or university in its effort to develop service-learning and international/intercultural education. Please include a description of the state of service-learning and international education on your campus

II. SERVICE Describe the types of volunteer service in which your students are or might be engaged, and the minimum number of hours you would require for a student to be considered for the distinguished service and learning certificate. Give the rationale for your selection of the number of hours. (For example, universities with full-time students will require a larger number of hours than those whose students are working full-time and going to school at night.)

III.   LEARNING Describe how you will judge the extent and quality of the learning that the candidate for the certificate has achieved through the service. (E.g., the learning may be measured through the awarding of academic credit and grades for studies related to service; it may be through a special essay, journal or interview with a committee; or other means.)

IV.   PROCEDURES FOR SELECTION Describe how you will select the students and agencies to receive the certificate. (E.g., who will make up the committee? Will the candidates apply, or will they be selected without application? How will the committee ensure that the most deserving candidates receive the certificate?)

V.   PUBLIC CEREMONY Describe the arrangements you have made to have the certificates awarded publicly, including a description of the event and naming the college official who has agreed to this arrangement.

Please submit the plan which answers the above questions, along with the enclosed application, to The International Partnership for Service-Learning.

APPENDIX V

NATIONAL SERVICE SCHEME OF INDIA

"NOT ME BUT YOU"
Profile of a Service-Learning Programme in India

1. Service-Learning for Global Citizenship

1.1 Those who live in the 21st century will have dual citizenship—one, each person's national citizenship and the other the global citizenship. The former is a legal status represented by documents such as the passport while the other is more a set of personality traits, attitudes and values operating in the relationships with peoples of other cultures and countries. Learning is also bound to become global learning, multi-disciplinary, trans-disciplinary, intercultural and international. Such a future scenario calls for intensive and proactive transformation of education, of which a major component can be service-learning, the symbiosis of academic study and community service, the combination of the word of the world, the linking of the classroom and the social laboratory outside, the fusion of reflection and action-praxis.

2. Indian Educational System

2.1 The Indian educational system comprises over 228 universities, 1770 professional educational institutions, over 8000 colleges of general education, 102,183 high schools/higher secondary schools, 176,772 middle schools and 598,354 primary schools according to the 1997 statistics. In the higher education sector, there are about 7 million students, which is less than 6% of the relevant college-going age group. This implies that about 94% of the 18-23 age group are outside the purview of post-secondary education. However, since the voting age has been reduced to 18 years, this principal segment of the population, whether inside the campus or outside, play a decisive role in democratic decision making on national governance. The character and quality of higher education received by the college-university student population have an important bearing on the nation's destiny and its quality of life.

3. National Service Scheme - Origin and Objectives

3.1 The major service learning Organisation in India is the National Service Scheme (NSS), which was planned and implemented by the Government of India in 1969. NSS is based on the concept of voluntarism and has a membership of over 1.5 million students and 10,000 programme officers. Since India became free from colonial domination in 1947, the idea that young men and women in colleges should undergo compulsory social service was gathering momentum.

In 1958, a Committee under the chairmanship of Dr. C.D. Deshmukh was set up to study the proposal and it recommended obligatory national service ranging from 9 to 12 months for all students after high school education and entering the college or university. However, this proposal could not be implemented due to financial constraints and the difficulty in making the additional period of time part of the college/university curricula. The Education Commission headed by Dr. D.S. Kothari (1964-66) strongly recommended the participation of students in community development projects. This recommendation led to the evolution of the National Service Scheme in 1969.

3.2 The Kothari Commission report pointed its finger at the "increasing gulf between the educated and the uneducated classes, between the intelligentsia and the masses" for which the existing educational system was held responsible. According to the Commission the intelligentsia should try to become "a real service-group striving to uplift the masses and to resist the temptation to become a parasitical group living for itself and perpetuating its own privileged decisions." Education should remain close to the people instead of tending to move away from them. In order to achieve this goal the Commission recommended that "some form of social and national service should be made obligatory for all students and to form an integral part of education at all stages. Hopefully this could become an instrument to build character, improve discipline, inculcate a faith in the dignity of manual labour and develop a sense of social responsibility."

3.3   The goal of the NSS has been spelt out as follows:

"The goal of the National Service Scheme should be education through community service. The purpose should be to enrich the student's personality and deepen his understanding of the social environment in which he lives. It should help the student to develop an awareness and knowledge of social reality, to have a concern for the well being of the community, to undertake appropriate activities designed to tackle social problems and to promote welfare. The student's self development should be the ultimate objective of the Scheme."

3.4   The National Service Scheme has the objective of enabling the participating students to:
i.   Understand the community in which they work;
ii.   Understand themselves in relation to their community;
iii.   Identify the needs and problems of the community and involve them in problem solving process;
iv.   Develop among themselves a sense of social and civic responsibility;
v.   Utilise their knowledge in finding practical solution to individual and community problems;
vi.   Develop competence required for group-living and sharing of responsibilities;
vii.   Gain skills in mobilising community participation;
viii.   Acquire leadership qualities and democratic attitude;
ix.   Develop capacity to meet emergencies and natural disasters; and
x.   Practice national integration and social harmony.

3.6   Features of NSS: The motto of National Service Scheme is "NOT ME BUT YOU," which emphasizes cooperative living, mutual help and respect for other people. All activities of NSS are based on this principle of subordinating personal and selfish interests to community interests and social wellbeing. The symbol of NSS is a wheel taken from an ancient monument still existing at the Konark Sun Temple in Orissa. According to an NSS document, the wheel portraits "the cycle of creation, preservation and release and signifies the movement in life across time and space." It also stands for "the progressive cycle of life," for "continuity and change," implying the continuous striving of NSS for social transformation and upliftment. The NSS badge has got on it embossed the NSS symbol, a wheel with eight bars representing the twenty four hours. It is clarified that the badge is a constant reminder to the student who wears it to be in perpetual readiness for service. The badge has red and navy blue colours. September 24 is celebrated as the "NSS day" every year. NSS has a ceremonial anthem, which is sung on important occasions of celebrations.

3.6   Enrollment: In 1969, NSS began with an enrollment of 40,000 students and in 1998-99, the enrollment went up to 1.45 million. Of this 0.96 million are male and 0.49 female students. This growth has been quite impressive.

4.   Structure and Procedures

4.1   At the college level there is a "Programme Officer," who is a college teacher, who has received special training in working with youth and organising service-learning activities. The number of programme officers in a college varies according to the number of student volunteers which is usually 100-120. The student volunteers are enrolled from among the college students based on their aptitude in community service and leadership skills. The programme officer and the student volunteers work in the context of the community around the college. Thus the students, the programme officer and the community are the basic components of NSS. Learning and community service are integrated in such a way that they supplement each other. Students get skill and experience in planning and executing development projects and other social service benefits such as better basic education, health care and civic services, while the community receives social development inputs.

4.2   NSS activities include two major types - (a) regular NSS activities and (b) special camping programmes. Regular NSS activities are undertaken by students in the campus or the adopted villages during weekend or after college hours. Under special camping programme, the volunteers participate in camps of ten days' duration during holidays, interacting and working with the local community on particular projects.

4.3 Normally a student volunteer has to engage in 120 hours of work in an academic year. Out of this, 20 hours are set apart for orientation, field visits etc.; 30 hours for work on the campus and 70 hours for community service in adopted villages/urban slums. On successful completion of the target hours and activities, the volunteers receive a certificate and other recognition useful to them in their future career.

4.4 The NSS programme is financed by the Government of India and the State Governments. A specified sum per student is allocated to meet the cost of training, activities, boarding and lodging during the camps, transport, incidentals etc. There are NSS regional centres in various States and national headquarters located in the Department of Youth Affairs and Sports, within the Ministry of Human Resource Development of the Government of India. Each University has an "NSS Cell" to coordinate the activities in the colleges affiliated to it. A Programme Coordinator administers the University NSS Cell. At the college level, a member of the teaching faculty who is less than 40 years of age at the time of the selection functions as the "Programme Officer." Advisory committees at the college, university, state and national levels guide and monitor the progress of the scheme. At the beginning of the academic year, each college unit of NSS prepares a calendar of activities with detailed planning including enrollment, constitution of college level Advisory Committee, orientation of volunteers, regular activities, evaluation, special camp and celebration of national events. Each volunteer is encouraged to maintain a work diary to record his or her accomplishments, time and date of activity, problems encountered and plans for the future.

4.5 The National Service Scheme activities are regularly monitored and evaluated at various levels. The feedback from such evaluation is communicated to the functionaries and volunteers for improving the performance.

5. Learning through Service - Areas of Concern

5.1 Education is construed as a process of human formation, which equips an individual with the knowledge, skills, values and attitudes required to lead a life of fulfillment and self-actualisation. The school and the college foster the intellectual, spiritual, physical and aesthetic facilities of the individual so as to make him or her productive and useful to oneself and society. However, this does not imply a totally individualistic, upward growth of a person towards self-aggrandizement. It is expected that the person will grow not only vertically but horizontally also, towards his or her fellow-beings in society, to all forms of life, animals and plants, to the entire Creation. Education is not merely a process of understanding the reality, physical, natural, biological or psychological, but also transforming the reality by intelligent application of human skills and creativity. The bottom line and the impact of education in a nation or the world would be not merely improved careers, enhanced personal incomes multiplied GNPs or spiralling stock markets, but also the sum total of human happiness and well being, the total quality of life enjoyed by the humankind, satisfaction of basic needs by each and every person and the integrity of the environment and life-supporting systems of Nature.

5.2 The progress of "learning through service" through the national service programmes are oriented to the above stated philosophy of education. The activities of NSS at the micro and macro levels are geared to this objective and some of them are listed below for the sake of illustration.

> Work with Children - Street children; handicapped and retarded children, abandoned babies, children in forced labour; work in creches.

> Gender Justice - Prevention of violence against women, denial of equality to women, and discrimination against women; training in legal rights of women; skill training for women, advocacy for women's rights.

Environmental Conservation - Minimising extinction of species; protection of ecosystem and biodiversity; preservation of rare animals such as tiger, elephant, giraffe; lion etc.; protection of forests especially rain forests with their rich irreplaceable flora and fauna; tree plantation campaigns; popularisation of use of non-conventional energy; prevention of soil erosion and work for soil conservation.

Social Development - Study of poverty and its causes; social analysis; avoiding untouchability towards depressed groups in society, discrimination based on class, caste or creed; empowerment of the poor socially, economically and politically so that they enjoy full civic rights; construction of low-cost houses for the homeless.

Human Rights Education - Enabling each citizen to exercise the rights, guaranteed by the Universal Declaration of Human Rights.

Campaign Against Alcohol, Drugs, AIDS and Tobacco - Sensitising children, youth and adults about the pernicious effects of alcohol, drugs, tobacco and AIDS; providing relief and rehabilitation to those who are afflicted by them.

Village Adoption - Selection and adoption of specific villages for intensive social development and caring through inputs such as literacy, health care, modernised road systems, drinking water, afforestation, political education, local self government and improved quality of life.

Health Care - Basic health care training for rural population, slum dwellers, school children, college students and other vulnerable groups; vaccination against polio, hepatitis, tuberculosis etc.; providing mid-day meals to school children; blood donation; construction of sanitary latrines, cleaning of village ponds and wells.; population education- visit to hospitals to help patients in letter writing, reading and counseling; help to physically and mentally handicapped persons.

Adult Education and Literacy - Under the "Education for All" project, the NSS volunteers organise and conduct literacy classes for drop-out children and illiterate adults in the evenings and during holidays on regular basis.

Mobile Libraries - Books, journals and other reading materials are taken in vehicles into remote areas and homes.

Prison Ministry - NSS volunteers visit prisoners to conduct literacy and continuing education classes; they also participate in the celebration of important religious festivals, cultural entertainment programmes, yoga training in the prisons.

Disaster Relief - At the time of floods, drought, cyclones, earthquake and other natural disasters, NSS volunteers rush to the scene and provide much needed relief and rehabilitation services.

Civic Duties - NSS volunteers participate in training the public in traffic rules, traffic control, voters' education, construction and repair of roads; clearance of garbage and other polluting materials from public places; upkeep of historical monuments and cultural heritage.

Leadership Development - Regular training in leadership skills, public speaking, team work etc.

5.3   All such activities are undertaken with the help of non-governmental organisations in the locality, civic bodies and other local organisations.

6.   Conclusion

6.1   NSS has responded to a vital need of the educational system in India by activating the third dimension of higher education, community service and combining it with the other two dimensions, teaching-learning and research. It is hoped that the number of students opting to join NSS will increase substantially in coming years. Interlinking this national project with service-learning programmes in other countries will impart a global character and flavour to its agenda.

Dr. Mani Jacob
General Secretary
All India Association for Christian Higher Education &
Secretary General
Associations of Christian Colleges and Universities
International Ecumenical Forum